THE Vegetarian
FACTFINDER

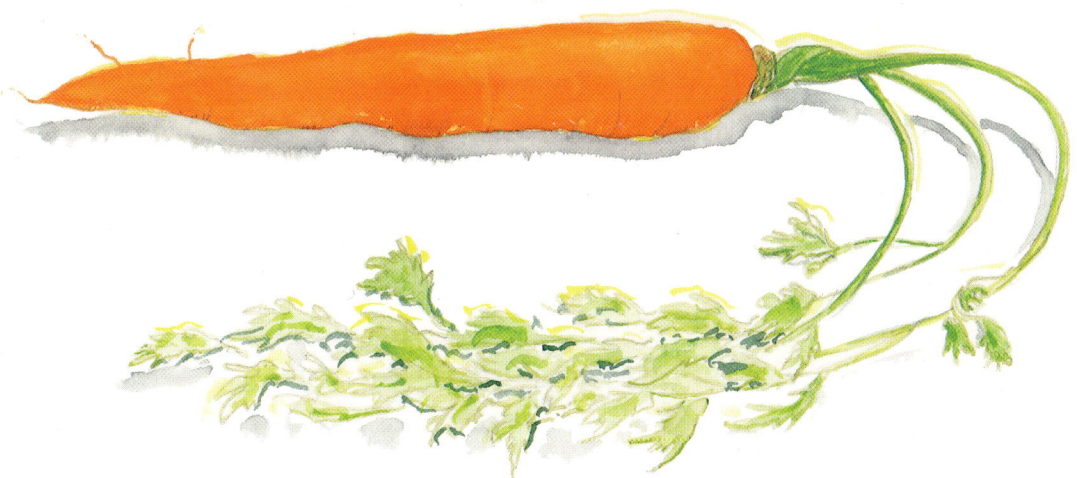

by **Ellen Klavan**

with illustrations by
Adrienne Hartman

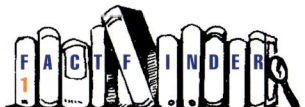

THE LITTLE BOOKROOM
NEW YORK

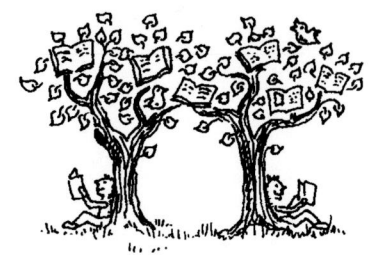

THE LITTLE BOOKROOM

Published by The Little Bookroom
5 St. Luke's Place, New York NY 10014 (212) 691-3321 fax (212) 691-2011
Copyright © 1996 by Ellen Klavan
Illustrations © 1996 by Adrienne Hartman
Design: Angela Hederman

The Little Bookroom acknowledges with appreciation the contributions of
Kerry Fried, Ursula Doyle, Claire Copley Eisenberg and The Little Bookboy, Richard Upchurch
Quote from DICK GREGORY'S NATURAL DIET FOR FOLKS WHO EAT by Dick Gregory
Copyright © 1973 by Richard Claxton Gregory
Reprinted by permission of HarperCollins Publishers, Inc.
Manufactured in Hong Kong by South China Printing Company (1988) Ltd.

The **FACTFINDER** series, published by The Little Bookroom,
explores a variety of non-fiction subjects of interest to children.
All rights reserved, which includes the right to reproduce this book or portions thereof in any form whatsoever.

Library of Congress Catalog Card Number: 96-76080
First Printing, June 1996

NOTE: The Little Bookroom was unable to obtain a CIP for this title so the following cataloging information was designed by the publisher to assist in cataloging. The reference has been designed for school libraries using Sears List of Subject Headings.

Klavan, Ellen
The Vegetarian Factfinder/Ellen Klavan; Illustrator Adrienne Hartman
"Factfinder" series #1

Summary: Discusses historical, religious, environmental and cultural issues of vegetarianism as well as why people become vegetarians and definitions of the choices involved in the lifestyle.
ISBN 0-9641262-1-4
1. Vegetarianism 2. Diet - Nutrition 3. Food - Natural
I. Hartman, Adrienne, illustrator. II. Title. III. Series.

613.2

For my parents
—E.K.

For that terrific duo:
Nicholas Stone, the vegetarian
and Leigh Hartman, the omnivore
—A.H.

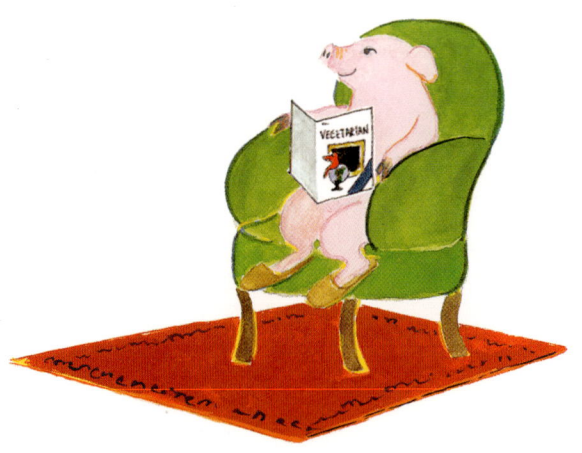

THE Vegetarian FACTFINDER

chapter 1 — what does vegetarian mean?
Page 3

The word "vegetarian" means different things to different people. It may mean giving up all meat or only certain meats. Or it may mean giving up "animal products," too, like milk, eggs and honey.

chapter 2 — why do people become vegetarians?
Page 9

Love of animals, religious inspiration, the quest for better health and concerns about the environment and world hunger are some of the reasons why people become vegetarians.

chapter 3 — where do vegetarians live?
Page 21

The world is full of vegetarians but most of them are "involuntary" vegetarians who can't afford meat. You'll also find vegetarians in countries where the major religion supports vegetarianism.

chapter 4 — who are vegetarians?
Page 25

From the Buddha to Leonardo to Mahatma Gandhi… here's a who's who of famous vegetarians.

chapter 5 — how do vegetarians stay healthy?
Page 41

Who's healthier, a vegetarian or a meat-eater? That depends on what they eat and how they get enough of the right things into their diets. Here's how healthy vegetarians stay that way.

Did you know?
Page 46
What's in a name?
Page 47

contents

"I'm a strict vegetarian—I don't eat meat or fish or any eggs or milk. My whole family is vegetarian. When my mother came out of college, she wanted to try a healthier lifestyle so she became a vegetarian. When she met my father, she told him about being a vegetarian and he became one too.

I've never tasted meat, so I guess I don't know what I'm missing. Sometimes I'm curious. I've always wanted to taste chicken because everyone says it's the best meat but I don't think I ever will. When I go to someone's house for the first time, I ask them to tell their parents that I don't eat meat so they know ahead of time and make something for me that I can eat. The problem is that it's not as good as the food we eat at home. My mother knows a lot of great recipes for meatless meals and I really like her cooking. But when I'm away from home I can usually get a salad or pasta."

Namik Minter
Age 12
Stone Mountain, Georgia

what does vegetarian mean?

You probably already know what the word *vegetarian* means. It describes a person who doesn't eat meat. But what is "meat," exactly? Does fish count? And what about the foods that animals produce, like eggs and milk? Even among people who call themselves vegetarians, there's a lot of disagreement over what the word *vegetarian* really means.

The Dos and Don'ts

One thing most vegetarians can agree about is what they **do** eat. They eat vegetables, of course, and fruits and lots of grains and legumes, otherwise known as beans and peas.

The difference of opinion comes in when you ask vegetarians what they **don't** eat.

Some vegetarians don't eat any animal. Cow, pig, sheep, chicken, alligator, fish, frog, ant—you name it, they don't eat it. Other vegetarians avoid eating most animals but do eat certain ones, like fish, for example.

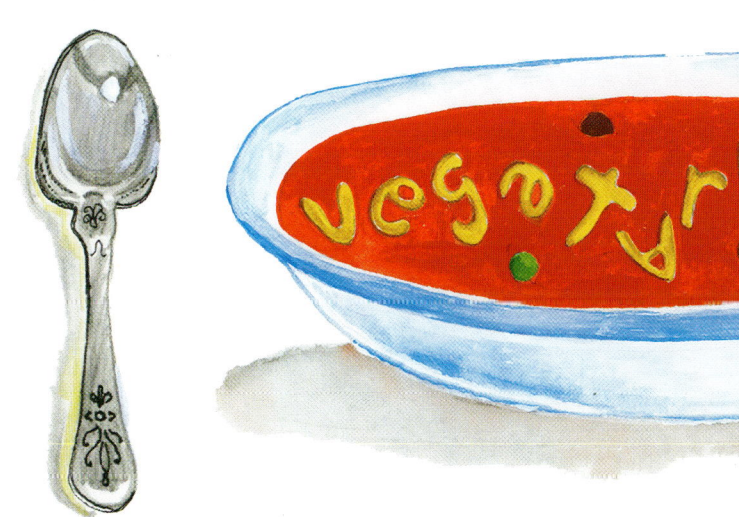

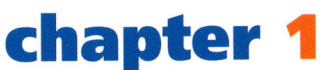

Different types of vegetarians

There are many different ways to be a vegetarian. Here are some of the most common:

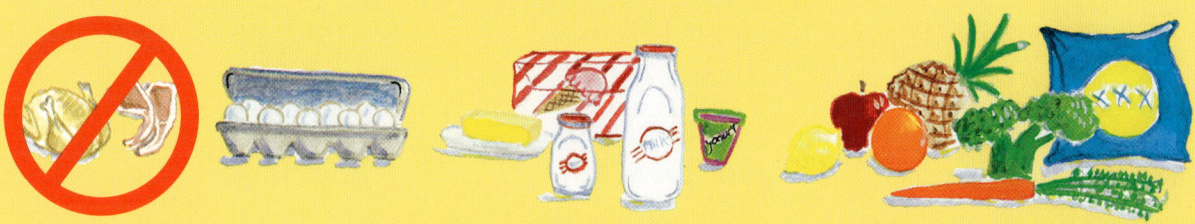

OVOLACTOVEGETARIAN: This is a big word that means that these vegetarians eat eggs (*ovo* in Latin) and milk products (*lacto* in Latin). Milk products include all kinds of milk from whole to skim, yogurt, cheese and ice cream.

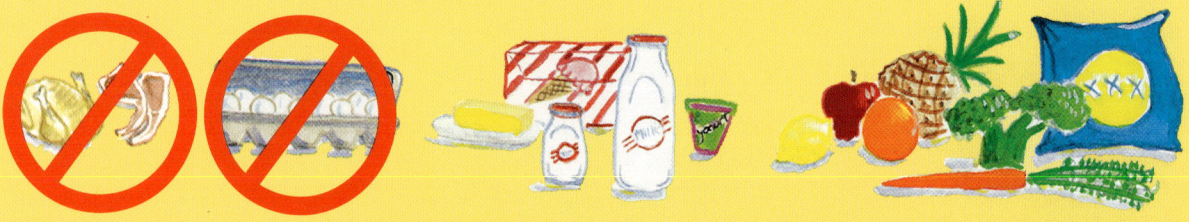

LACTOVEGETARIAN: You can probably guess—these vegetarians eat milk products but no eggs.

Some vegetarians—called *vegans*—don't eat any animal **or** any animal products. An animal product is anything a living animal makes. The list of animal products includes eggs from chickens, milk, yogurt, cheese and ice cream from cows, even honey from bees. Vegans also avoid wearing or using anything made from animal products—like leather shoes, down quilts and beeswax candles.

A Way of Life

To many people, being a vegetarian is more than a way of eating; it's a way of life. Often, vegetarians

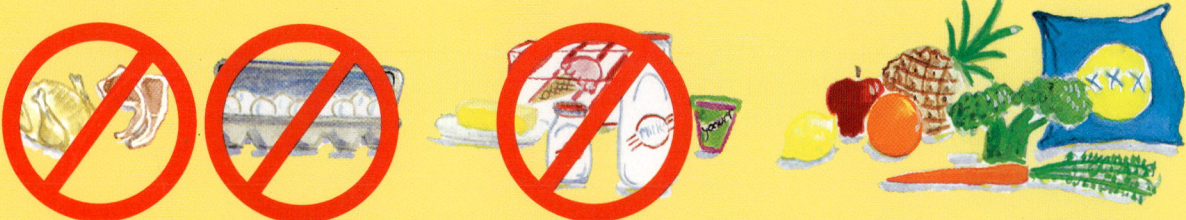

VEGAN (pronounced veé-gun): These vegetarians don't eat anything that comes from an animal. Vegans are sometimes called strict vegetarians because they make no exceptions to the meat-free rule.

Lots of people who call themselves vegetarians don't exactly fit into any of these categories. For instance, many people eat fish but no other meat products. Others eat fish and chicken but no "red meat" (beef, lamb or pork). And others call themselves "flexible," "casual" or "semi-" vegetarians—those are people who usually avoid meat but make exceptions from time to time.

make a solemn vow to themselves not to eat meat. These people may feel quite guilty—and even sick—if they make an exception.

Other vegetarians are less strict—they may choose to eat meat occasionally without feeling that they've broken a personal rule. Strict vegetarians might argue that those who eat meat occasionally aren't "real" vegetarians. Those who do eat meat may think strict vegetarians are too fussy. For the most part, though, vegetarians try to respect one another's views.

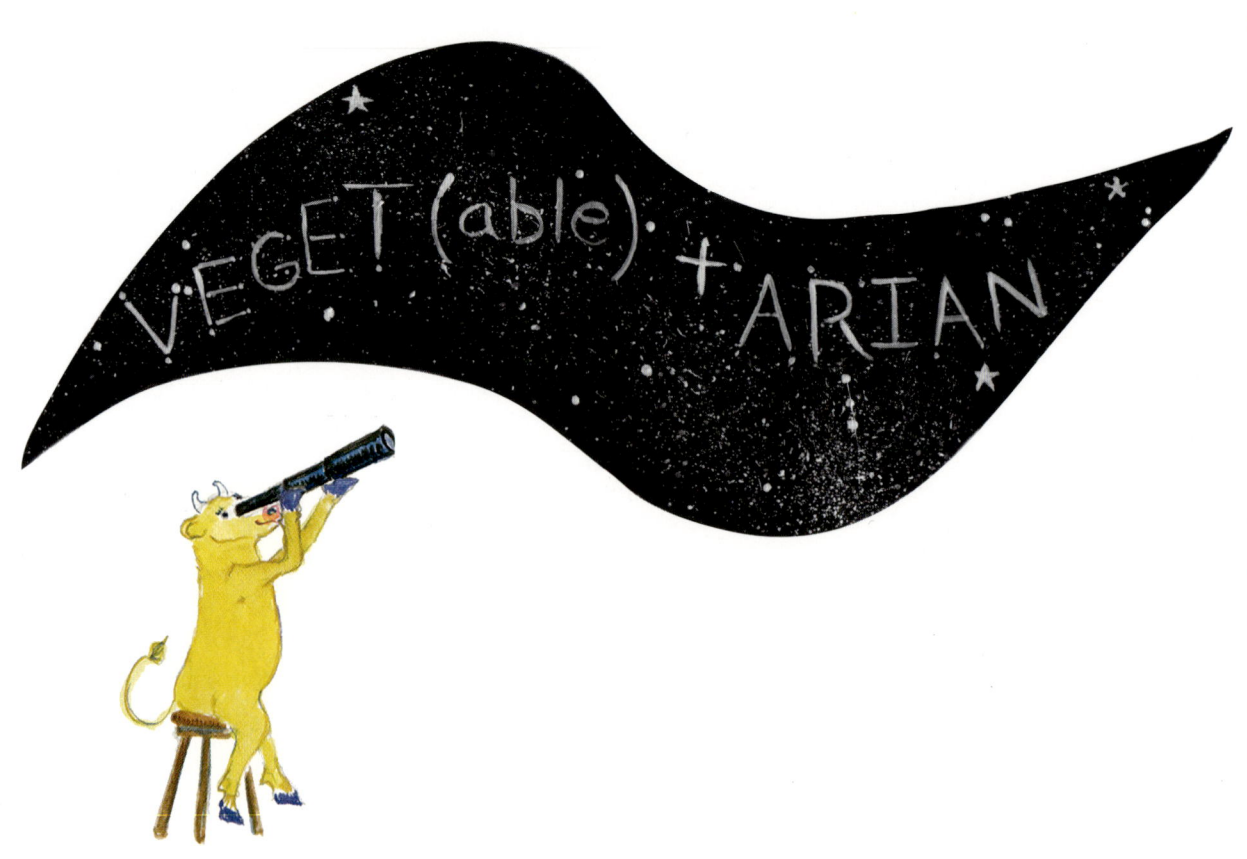

Take a look at the word vegetarian. It has two parts: *veget* and *arian*.

The first part, *veget-*, comes from the word vegetable. And that word in turn comes from the Latin word *vegere*, which means to enliven or bring to life. Just about everyone who chooses to be a vegetarian does so to improve the quality of life. As we'll see in the next chapter, some people become vegetarians to improve their bodies' health and maybe live longer as a result. Others want to save the lives of animals, protect the environment or improve the lives of hungry people around the world. Some people believe that being vegetarian enhances their spiritual lives.

The second part, *-arian*, means "believer" or "advocate." An advocate is someone who argues on behalf of a person or a cause. As we'll see, many vegetarians are people who believe passionately in the virtue of giving up meat. We'll meet men, women and children who are believers in and advocates for vegetarianism.

This book is neither for nor against a vegetarian way of life. Its purpose is to help you find out what vegetarianism is, why some people become vegetarians, where they live, who they are and how they do it. The rest—including thinking about whether you want to be a vegetarian—is up to you.

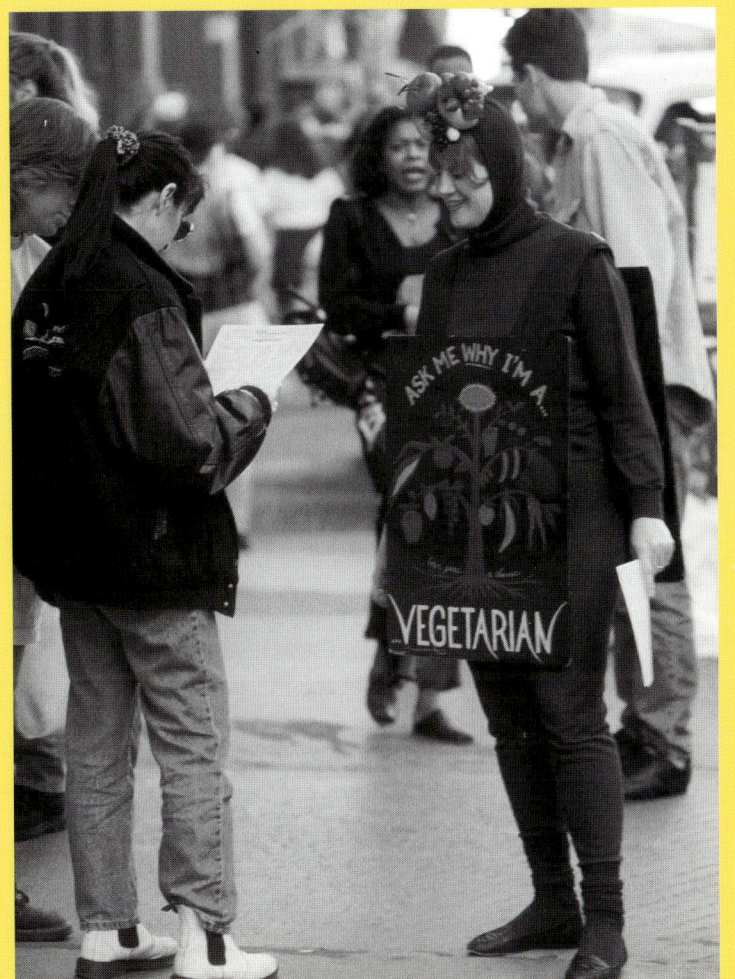

Angela Hederman

A vegetarian takes to the streets to convince others to give up meat

It takes a lot to get busy New Yorkers to slow down and pay attention. Vegetarian activist Pam Teisler-Rice wears a sandwich board and eye-catching costume to attract interest in her cause.

"I became a vegetarian six years ago when I was eight. I had tried once before but then I went to my favorite restaurant and I gave in. Then six years ago we went to France and we were walking through a meat market. I saw all the meat out in the open. There were cows' tongues and whole chickens with their heads still on and skinned rabbits—it was disgusting. Seeing it all there was horrible. And that's when I gave up meat for good.

At first my parents didn't like my becoming a vegetarian too much. They were concerned about my health and it was also inconvenient. My dad is on a different diet from everyone else and now I was too. But in time they realized that there's not much they can do about my being a vegetarian because I feel really strongly about it.

My mom's gotten used to me being a vegetarian. She buys me special vegetarian meals that she can heat up along with the rest of the family's dinner. And she's seen that I can eat sensibly as a vegetarian. I think I'm less of a nuisance about it now too. I don't expect as much from my mother. If she doesn't make something vegetarian, I can make something for myself or eat around the meat in the family's meal. It's still hard if we all go to a restaurant and there's no vegetarian meal on the menu. I may have to order two starters and I get annoyed and my parents get frustrated with me. But mostly they take it pretty well."

Nadia Tarazi
Age 14
London, England

why do people become vegetarians?

Give up hot dogs? Turn down fried chicken? Why would anyone do it?

To most of us, eating meat is as American as sitting down to roast turkey on Thanksgiving or barbecuing hamburgers for a Fourth of July picnic. So why do people choose to go without?

There are probably as many different answers to that question as there are vegetarians.

Here are some of the most common explanations:

Love of animals

For some vegetarians, it's as simple as this: they don't want to eat another living creature. Animals may not compose symphonies or build cars, but they are conscious, sensitive and —to varying degrees— intelligent beings. Pigs, for instance, are said to be as intelligent as dogs.

Some animal lovers find it hard to give up favorite foods like chicken and steak but they do it anyway because they believe it is wrong to eat meat. Other animal lovers say it's easy to give up meat— they may find the sight, smell and taste of meat disgusting.

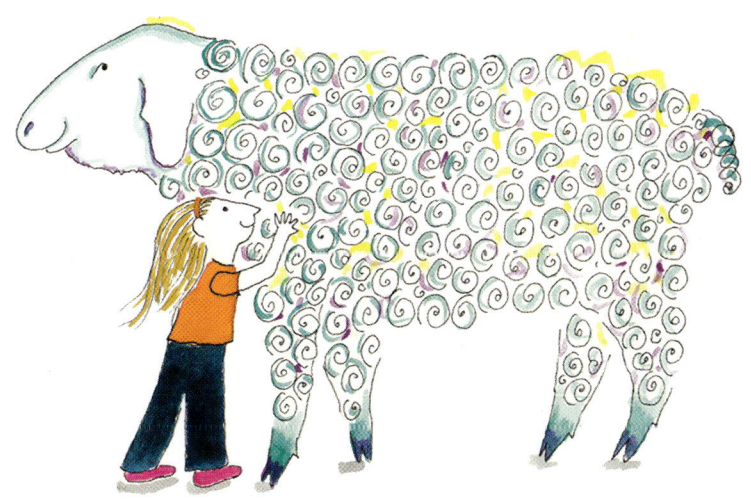

chapter 2

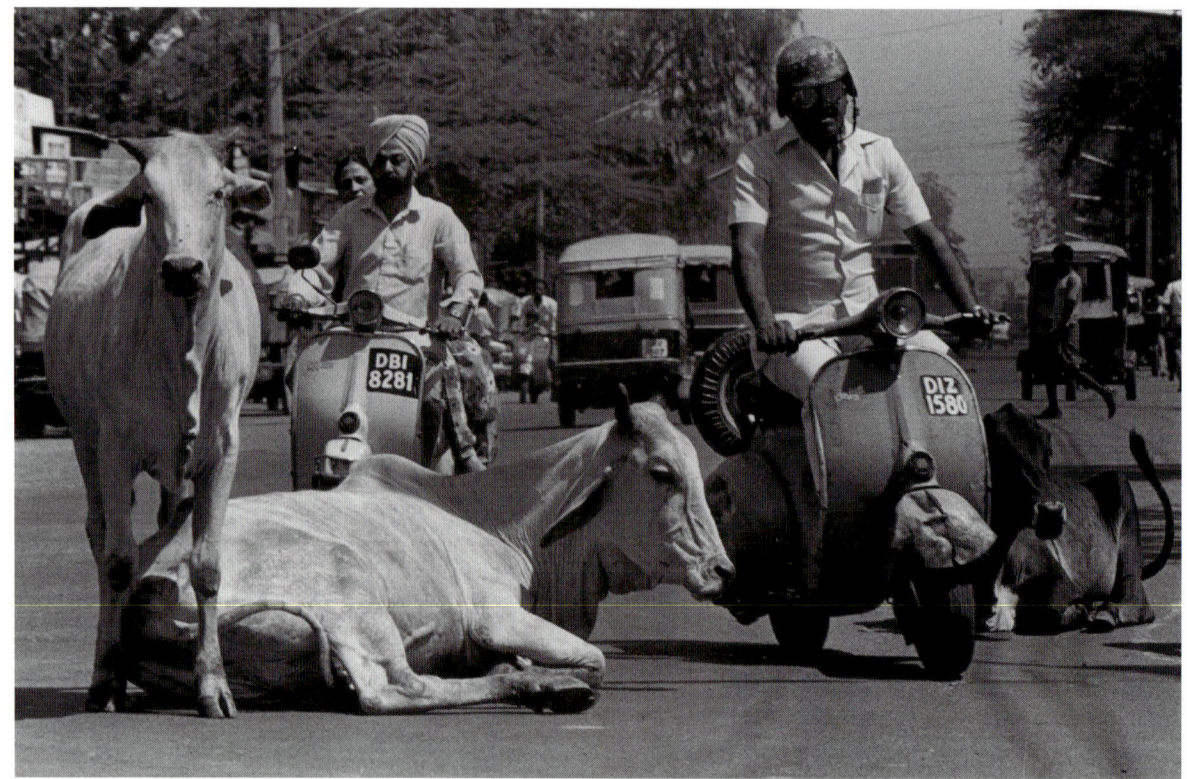

Reuters/Bettmann

Holy cow! *Hindus believe the cow is the most sacred of all animals. In India, where the population is about 80% Hindu, cows are cherished, petted and allowed to wander wherever they wish, as shown above. Most Hindus wouldn't even consider moving a cow out of the way on a busy street, let alone eating one.*

Religious reasons

Some people become vegetarians because their religions require or urge them to. Many Hindus and Buddhists, for example, are vegetarians and so are some Christians and members of other religious groups. You can find out more about religious vegetarians on pages 27-32.

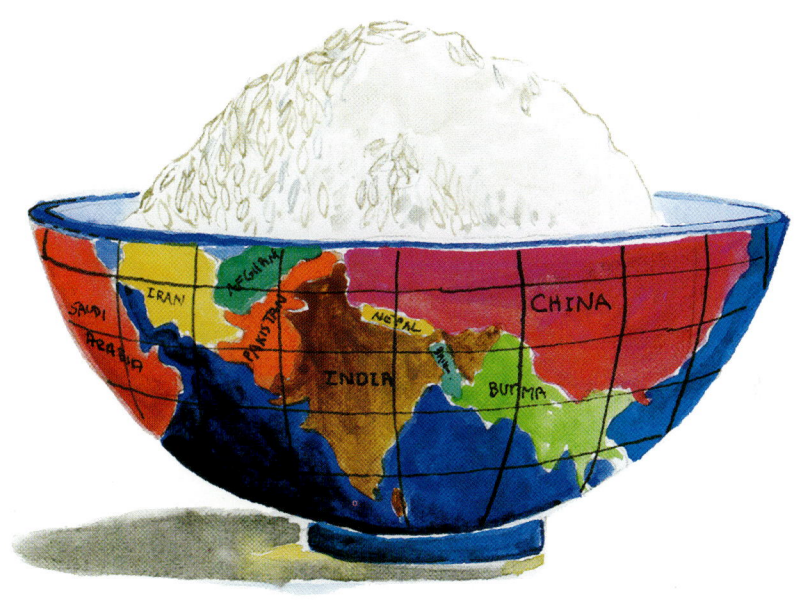

Concerns about world hunger

Rich countries, like America, spend lots of time and money on meat production. Every year we grow tons of grain and other non-meat foods just to feed animals we eventually kill and eat. The average cow eats sixteen pounds of grain and soy beans to produce every pound of meat that will be eaten.

Meanwhile, people in other countries around the world don't have enough to eat. Many people become vegetarians because they believe that if we weren't raising crops to feed animals we could be raising crops to feed hungry people all over the world. These vegetarians might not object to eating meat if they were sure that everyone in the world had enough to eat.

Concerns about cruelty to animals

Many vegetarians are horrified by the way animals who are raised in giant **factory farms** are treated. When animals are raised on this type of farm, the farmer's job is to produce as much meat as he can as cheaply as possible. He may have very little concern for the comfort or well-being of the animals he raises. Many vegetarians believe that factory-farmed animals are the victims of terrible cruelty.

On factory farms, chickens, cows, lambs and pigs spend their entire lives in over-crowded cages, often in spaces that are so small that they can't turn around or even lie down comfortably. These animals never see the light of day and are sometimes fed too little (because the farmer doesn't want to waste food on them) or too much (because the farmer wants to fatten them up).

The fate of young calves that are raised to become veal is especially sad. First, the farmer takes the calf away from its mother before it is weaned, something which is traumatic for both the cow and the calf. Then the calf is placed in an uncomfortably small cage and force-fed until it is fat enough for slaughter.

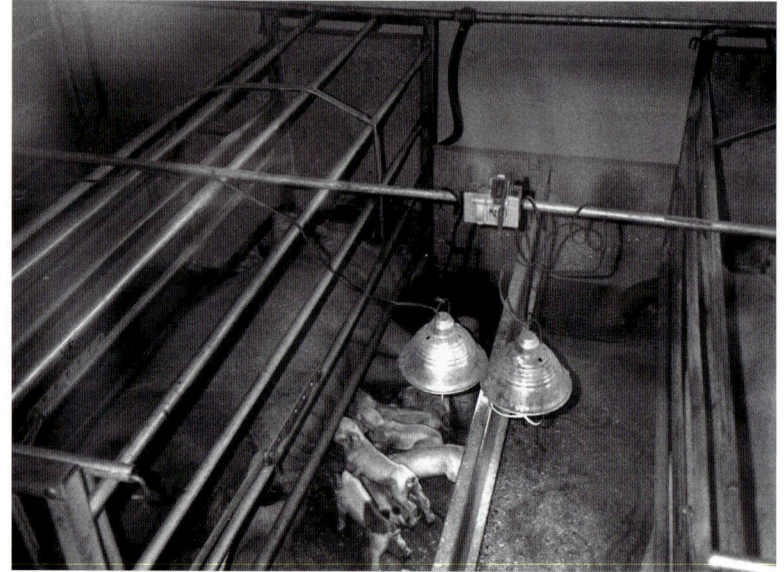

Humane Farming Association

A sad contrast. The factory-farmed mother pig, on the left, is isolated in a confining metal pen, separated from her young, while the pig at right receives tender loving care from her owner.

Cows that are kept for milking and chickens which lay eggs may also be mistreated.

Animals which are factory-farmed can become quarrelsome, and this creates difficulties for farmers. Some of their solutions add to the animals' suffering. For instance, to keep chickens from pecking one another, farmers cut off their beaks. To keep stressed pigs from biting each others'

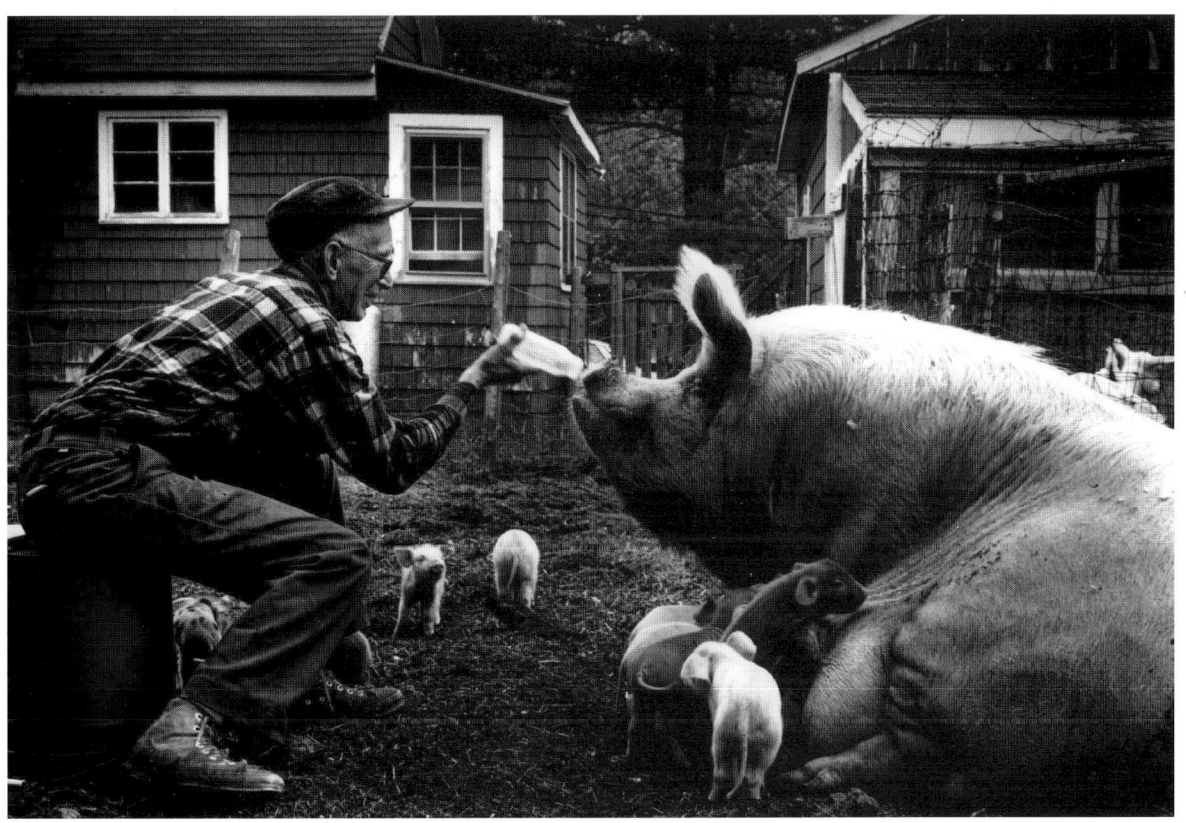

© 1993 Amy Kunhardt / Impact Visuals

tails, the tails are cut off.

Animals that are raised to be eaten must eventually be killed. In theory, the killing is handled quickly and painlessly. In practice, though, some slaughterhouses make the animals' deaths unnecessarily cruel and painful.

Some vegetarians eat fish because unlike farm animals most fish swim free in large bodies of water.

Other people who are concerned about the cruelty animals experience on factory farms choose to eat only "free-range" meat. This is a term used to describe animals which have been allowed to run free during their lives on the farm and were never crowded into cages.

Unfortunately, free-range meat is more expensive than factory-farmed meat so it is a luxury that most people can't afford.

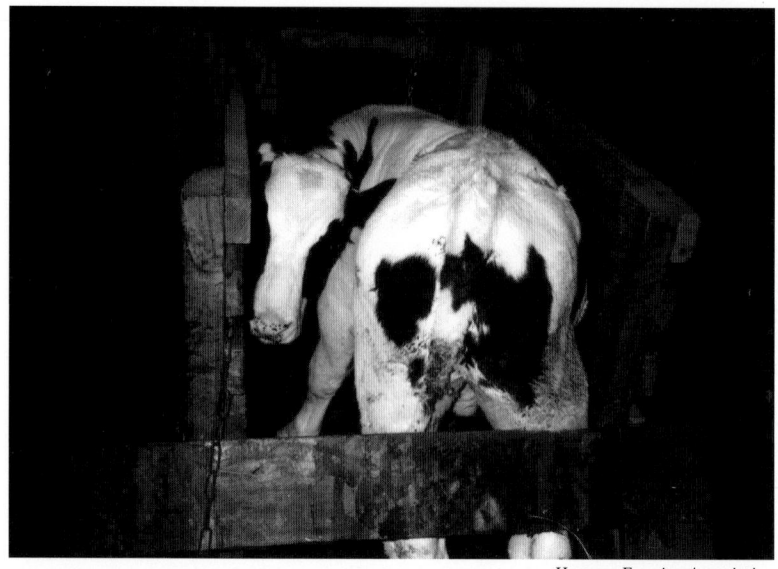

Humane Farming Association

Fat, weak and miserable: a veal calf at "home." *The calf is confined to a tiny cage so that it won't romp around and grow muscular. It is fed an unnatural diet that keeps its flesh pale and is denied water so that its only choice is to eat more and more liquid food.*

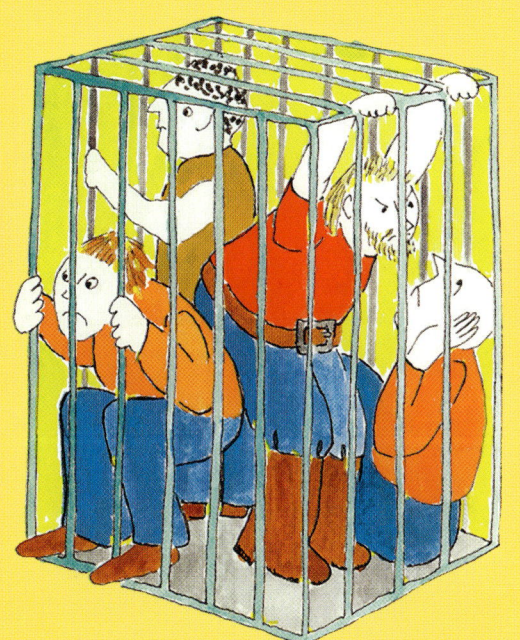
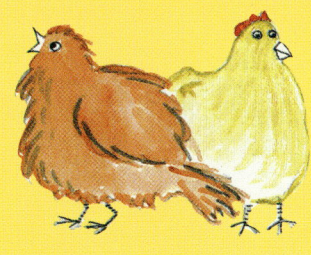

Trading places

WANTED: Four healthy adults to spend week in cage.

The men who answered English vegetarian Rebecca Hall's advertisement were in for a shock. She wanted them to spend a week crammed together into a cage only 40 inches square and 5 feet 3 inches high. That was the equivalent in human terms, she figured, to the cages factory-farmed chickens spend their lives in.

To make the experience even more lifelike, she put the cage in a windowless shed lit by bright electric lights and played a tape of human beings laughing and screaming. There was no toilet in the cage and the men had to eat brown rice and beans delivered by an automatic food dispenser.

It wouldn't be easy, but the four men who signed on for the job thought it would be worth the approximately $3,750 Rebecca had offered to pay each of them for their week in the cage. She never had to pay them though...after just eighteen hours in the cage, all four men bailed out!

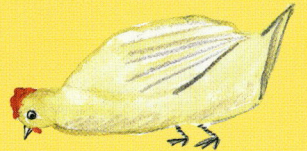

Health concerns

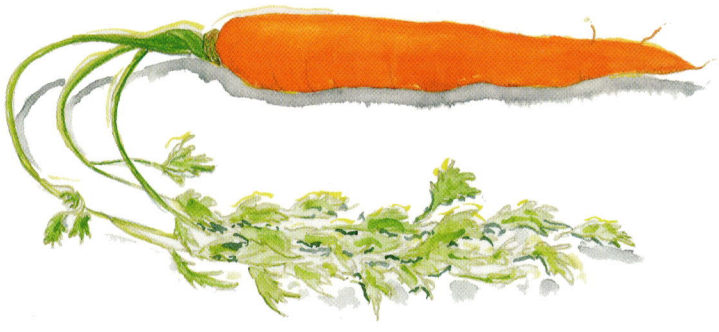

A great many vegetarians give up meat because they believe they will be healthier without it. Here's why:

Fat and cholesterol

Doctors now agree that too much fat and cholesterol is harmful. One of the main sources of fat is meat and the *only* sources of cholesterol are meat and animal products. So it makes sense to cut back on these foods as a way of staying healthy. Everyone—especially children and teenagers—needs *some* fat, though, and vegetarians need to be careful to include a little fat in their diets.

Of course, becoming a vegetarian is not the only way to eat a low-fat diet. In fact, vegetarians who eat a lot of cheese may be eating a more fatty diet than non-vegetarians who eat small amounts of lean meat.

Hormones and antibiotics

There are other health reasons, besides fat, to avoid meat. Many farmers feed their animals hormones, which make the animals grow faster. The problem with this from the humans' point of view is that the hormones are stored up in the animals' flesh and we end up eating them along with our burgers or chicken nuggets.

Farmers also feed farm animals antibiotics (like the antibiotics you may take if you have an earache) to prevent infection. The problem with this is that overusing antibiotics may

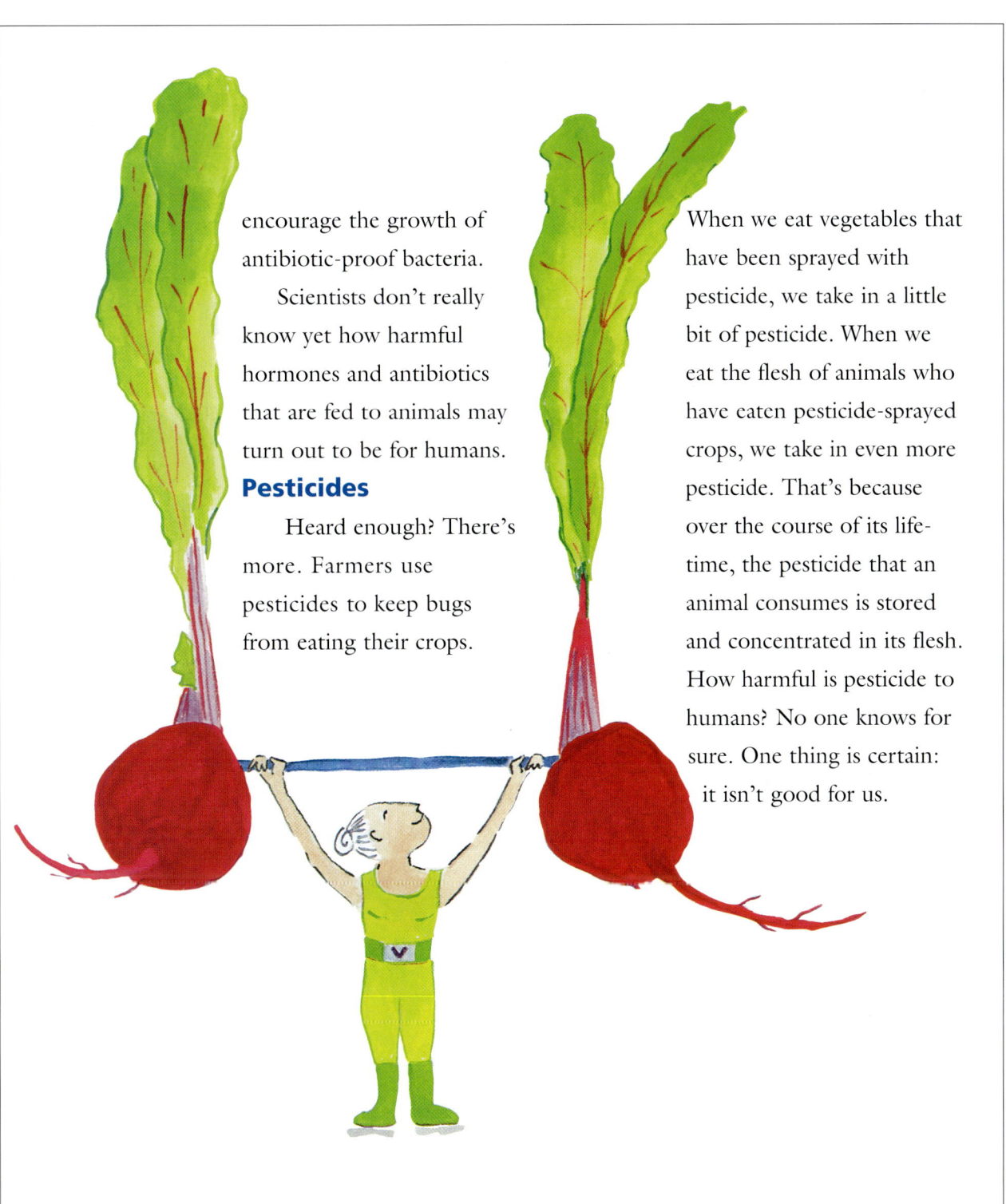

encourage the growth of antibiotic-proof bacteria.

Scientists don't really know yet how harmful hormones and antibiotics that are fed to animals may turn out to be for humans.

Pesticides

Heard enough? There's more. Farmers use pesticides to keep bugs from eating their crops.

When we eat vegetables that have been sprayed with pesticide, we take in a little bit of pesticide. When we eat the flesh of animals who have eaten pesticide-sprayed crops, we take in even more pesticide. That's because over the course of its lifetime, the pesticide that an animal consumes is stored and concentrated in its flesh. How harmful is pesticide to humans? No one knows for sure. One thing is certain: it isn't good for us.

Concerns about the environment

For many people, vegetarianism is part of a larger ideal of living in harmony with the earth. They are concerned that farm animals are literally eating up some of the world's most important resources.

There are two ways to feed animals that you are growing for slaughter and each of them uses up resources. The first is to feed them grains and soybeans that have been harvested from the earth. But doing this uses up fuels (used by farm equipment)

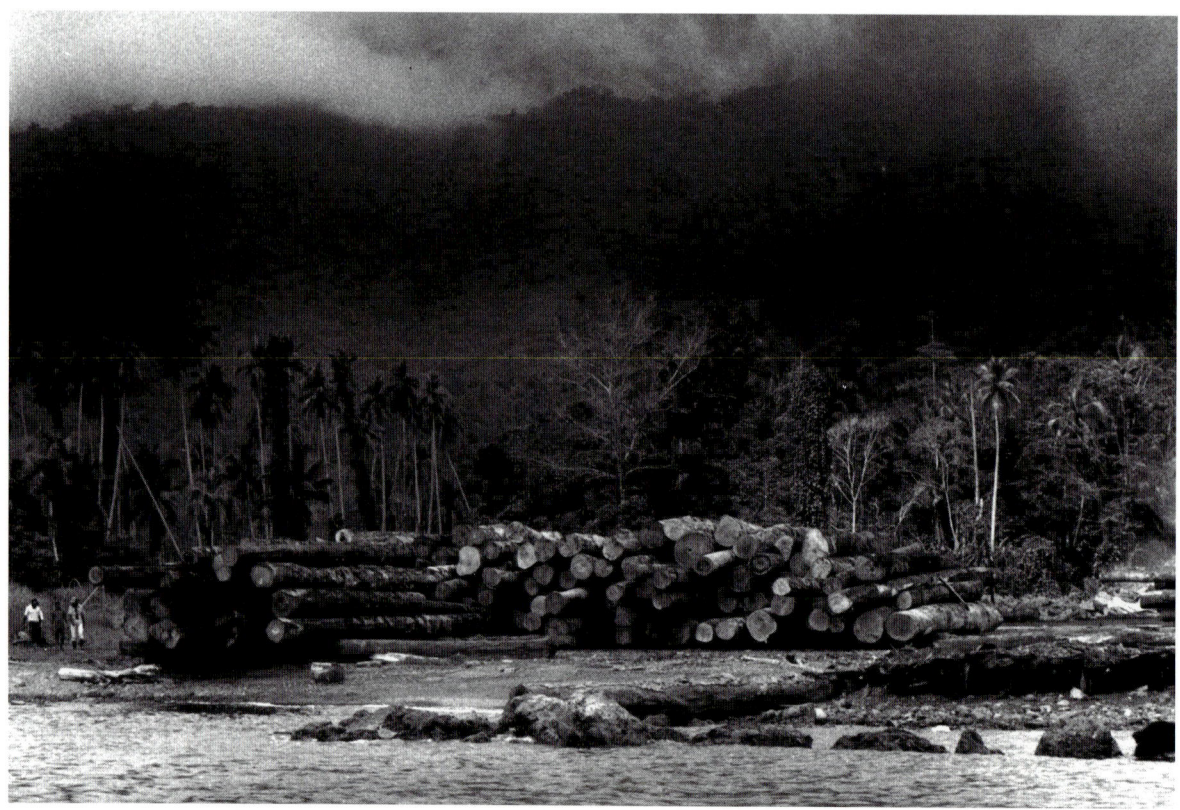

© Greenpeace / Dorreboom

Making way for cattle: *In Papua New Guinea, a rainforest is cut down to create new grazing land.*

and water (needed to water the crops) and wears away the soil. Nitrates from fertilizers also pollute underground water supplies.

The other method is to allow the animals to graze, which means turning them loose on open pasture land to eat the grasses which grow there naturally. Here the problem is that after a while, pastures become "overgrazed" and the land becomes useless. Often farmers cut down forests to create more grazing land. This is one of the reasons that we are losing some of the world's important rainforests.

If those weren't problems enough, there's also manure and — er — other emissions. When manure seeps into the water it causes water pollution. And the gases that livestock emit contribute to the greenhouse effect.

All of these problems are worse than ever before in human history because the twentieth century has produced more meat than ever before.

"I became a vegetarian two years ago. My mother and sister were both vegetarians and I heard them talking about a book they'd both read about the things they do to animals and I decided I wanted to be a vegetarian too.

I'd thought since I'd been eating meat for a long time it would be hard to go really quickly. So at first I stopped eating bacon and other food from pigs. Then I stopped eating beef and then chicken. At first it was hard but I told myself that I'd made a commitment and I had to stick to it. Now it's not hard any more.

I'm the only one of my friends who's a vegetarian. Some of my friends accept it but some of them ask weird questions. Like they'll say, "If you were trapped in a cave with no way out and there was a fifty pound slab of meat and nothing else to eat, would you eat it?" I just ignore them or tell them I don't want to talk about it."

Bruce Ho
Age 12
San Antonio, Texas

where do vegetarians live?

Besides the reasons for not eating meat described in the last chapter, there's one more reason why many people eat little or no meat. In fact, far more people are vegetarians —or partial vegetarians— for this reason than any other. The reason is: Meat is expensive. The vast majority of the world's vegetarians are **"involuntary"** vegetarians who can't afford to eat meat on a regular basis.

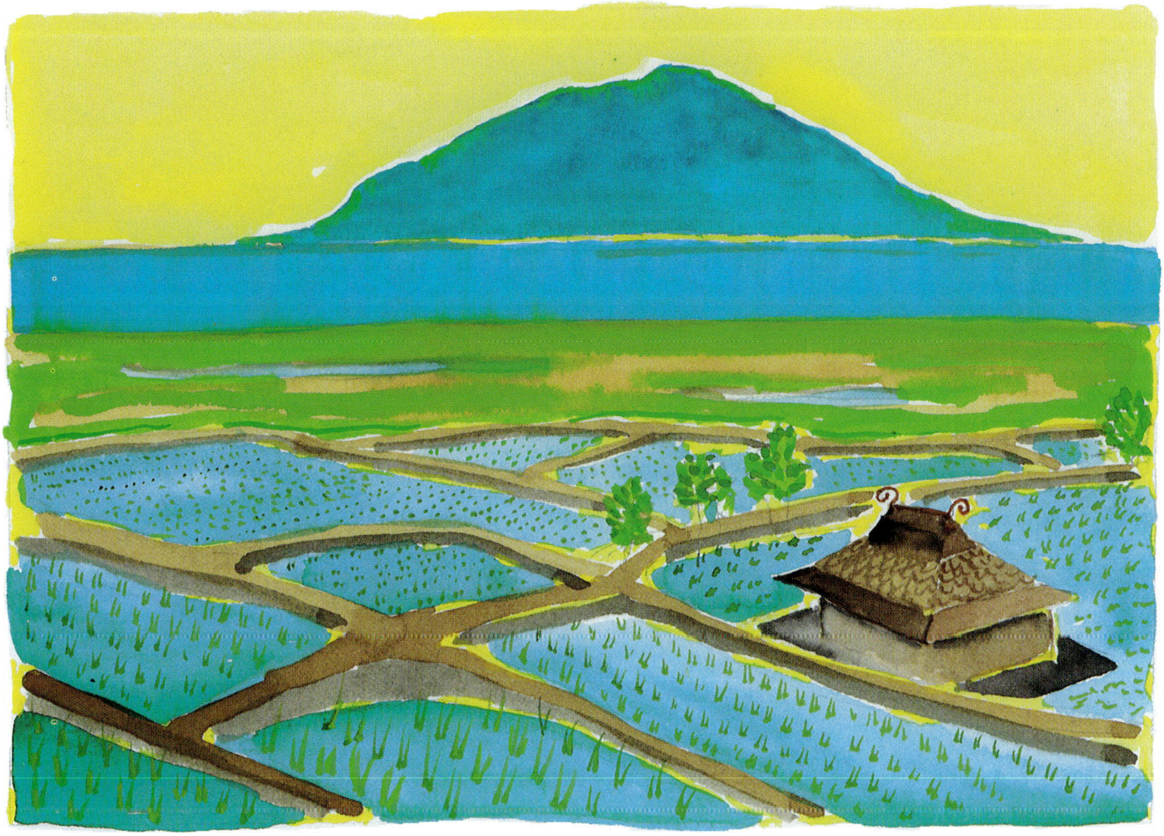

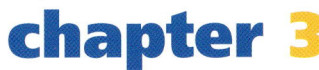

chapter 3

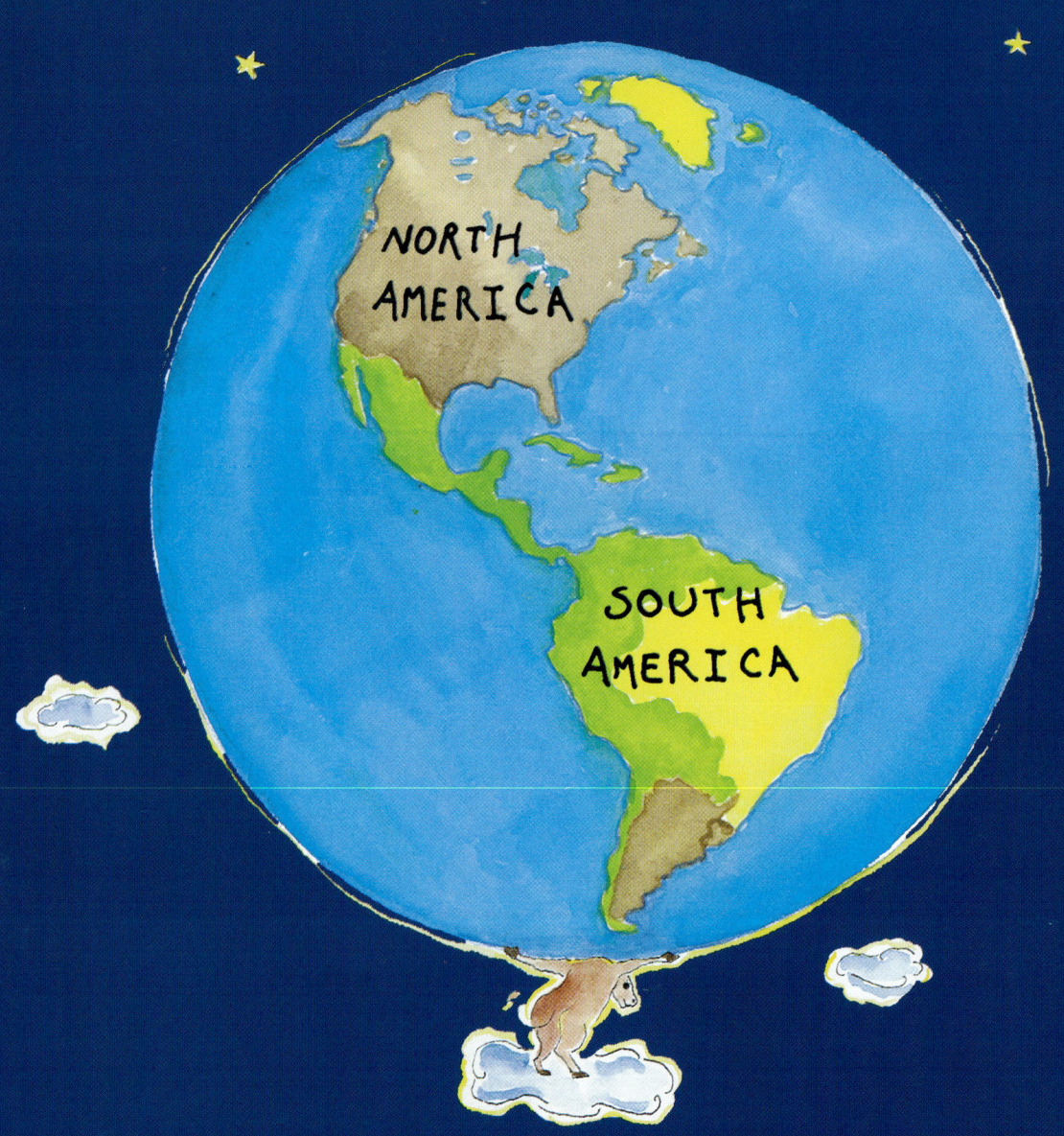

If you take a look at the maps on these two pages, you'll see that the countries where the most meat is eaten (the brown countries) tend to be those (like the United States) that are the wealthiest. Also, people tend to eat more meat in countries where meat is produced (like Argentina). Those where the least meat is eaten (the green countries) tend to be the poorest. Probably the second largest group of vegetarians—after involuntary

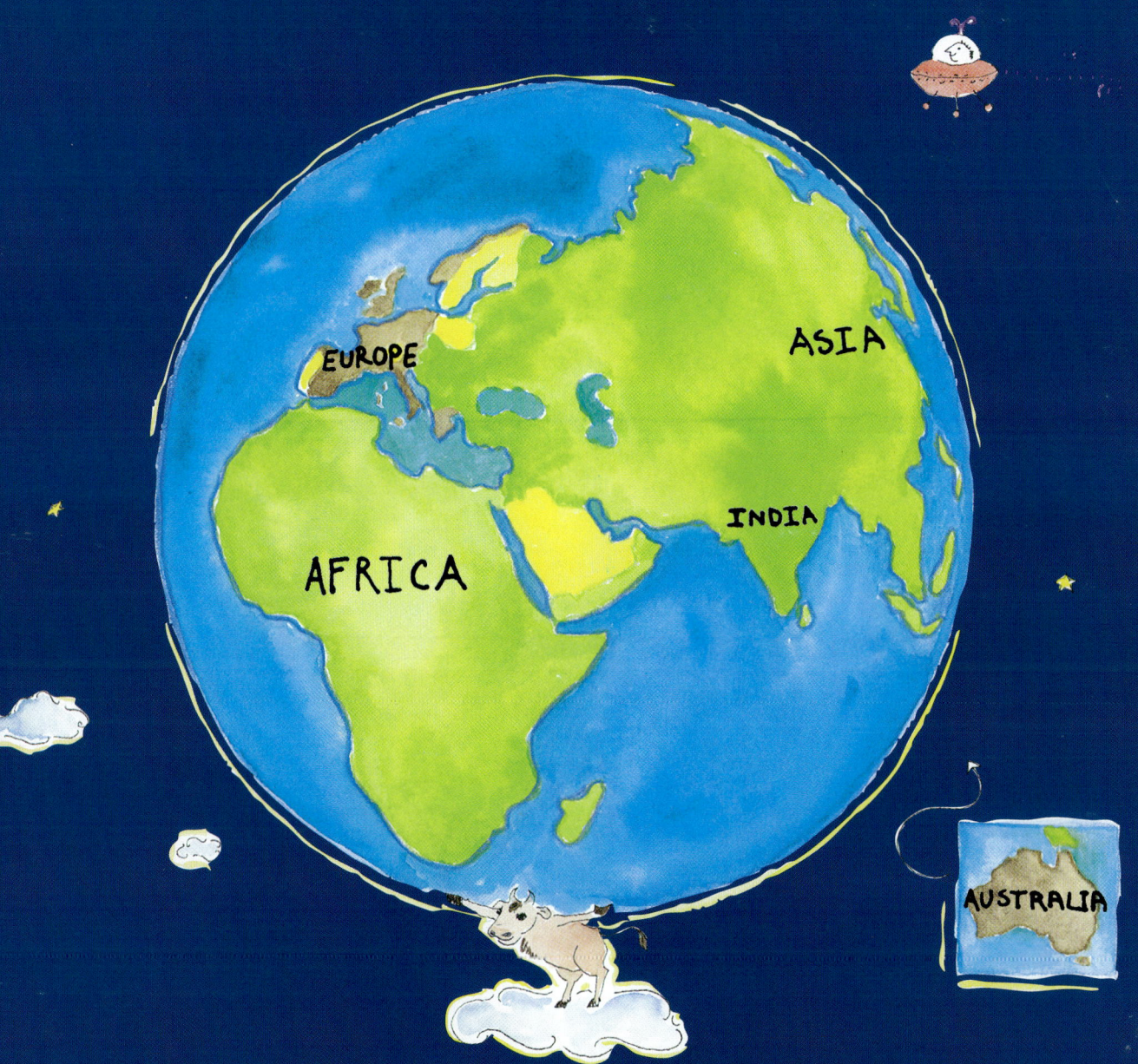

vegetarians—are those who avoid meat for religious reasons. India, for example, where Hinduism is widely practiced, is undoubtedly the world capital of vegetarianism. Other voluntary vegetarians (those who give up meat by choice) are scattered around the world but in relatively small numbers. By some estimates, 1% of the population of the United States and 5% of the population of the United Kingdom are vegetarians.

"When I was in fifth grade, I was given some chickens as pets. One day I came home from school and I was playing with the chickens and then I came in to dinner and there was chicken on my plate. That was a defining moment for me, the moment when I decided to become a vegetarian.

The first meat I gave up was chicken and then little by little I gave up other meat. Three years ago I became a strict vegetarian (vegan). Partly I did this because when I would try to tell other kids about being a vegetarian, they would challenge me and say, "Look, you're wearing leather," and things like that. And I thought, *they're right*. Also I visited an egg farm and saw—and heard—the chickens' suffering…it was overwhelming. I couldn't eat eggs after that.

I feel that this is the best way for people to live. I think that if other people had some of the experiences I have had they would agree. On the personal side, getting control over what you eat builds confidence. And then on the global side it's not just the issue of animals' welfare, it's issues of global hunger and waste—the environment is extremely important to me. Together, it just makes sense."

Marc Romanoff
Age 16
Narberth, Pennsylvania

who are vegetarians?

Meat-eating is as old as humankind. The first humans, like their cousins, the primates, ate meat when they could, although their diet consisted mainly of plant foods. As time went on, humans learned to hunt for animals and later to raise domesticated animals for food. It was only after humans settled in communities and developed language, culture and religion that anybody questioned the morality of eating meat.

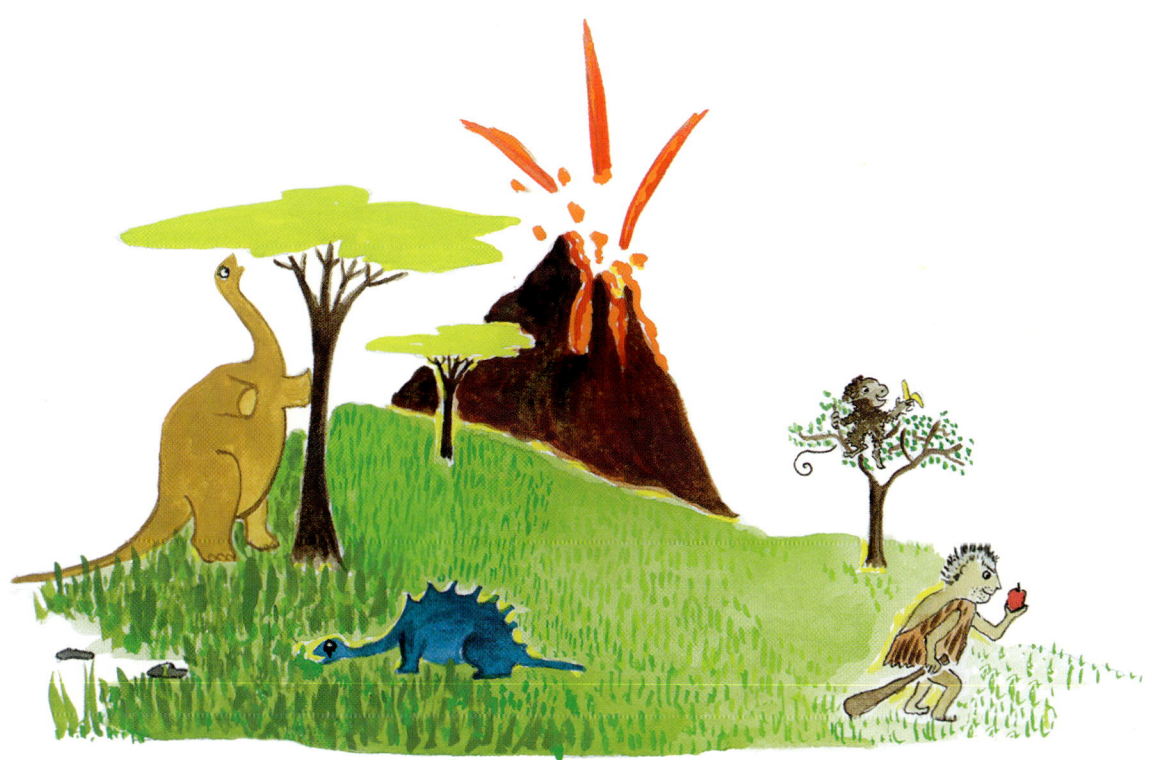

chapter 4

In fact, the conscious decision not to eat meat is a very human act. Although animals are apparently capable of kind and even heroic actions, they are not known to turn down food for moral reasons. It's hard to imagine a cheetah worrying about how a gazelle will feel when he bites into it. Dogs and cats don't show any concern for the souls of the ground meat they find in their feed bowls.

Human beings, though, think about right and wrong and question their own desires and motives. Unlike an animal, a human is capable of wanting something—a hamburger, for instance—but choosing not to have it for ethical or moral reasons.

Vegetarianism is part of the history of ideas.

ALBERT EINSTEIN
1879-1955

Our task must be to...(widen) our circle of compassion to embrace all living creatures and the whole of nature in its beauty.

Great minds sometimes think alike. Vegetarianism has fascinated some of the world's greatest intellectuals.

ISAAC BASHEVIS SINGER
1904-1991

To be a vegetarian is to disagree— to disagree with the course of things today. Starvation, world hunger, cruelty, waste, wars— we must make a statement against these things. Vegetarianism is my statement. And I think it's a strong one.

JEREMY BENTHAM
1748-1832

The question is not, Can they *reason?* Nor Can they *talk?* but Can they *suffer?*

Soul food: Religious vegetarians

For many vegetarians, avoiding meat is a matter of faith. These are some of the religions that practice vegetarianism:

Hinduism

Hinduism is one of the oldest religions in the world and one of the first to recommend vegetarianism. Hindus haven't always practiced vegetarianism—the idea evolved with the religion. But included right from the start of the religion were various ideas that led to a vegetarian way of life. Some of these ideas were:

- Early Hindus considered certain animals to be sacred—the elephant, the tiger and the cow.
- Early Hindus believed in reincarnation, the idea that a person's soul lived on, in another form, even after the person's body died. A soul might be reincarnated as a human, an animal or a god. According to this Hindu belief, killing an animal was just as bad as killing a human being because an animal's soul was the same as a human's soul.

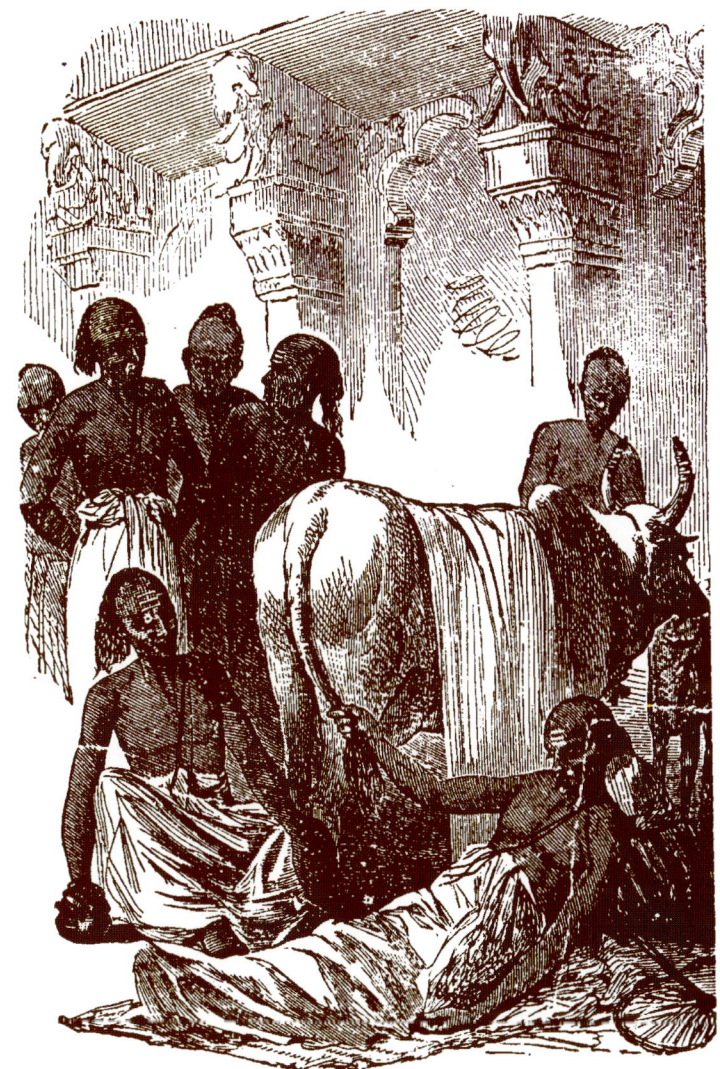

Divine intervention: *A dying Hindu holds the tail of a sacred cow so as to enter heaven.*

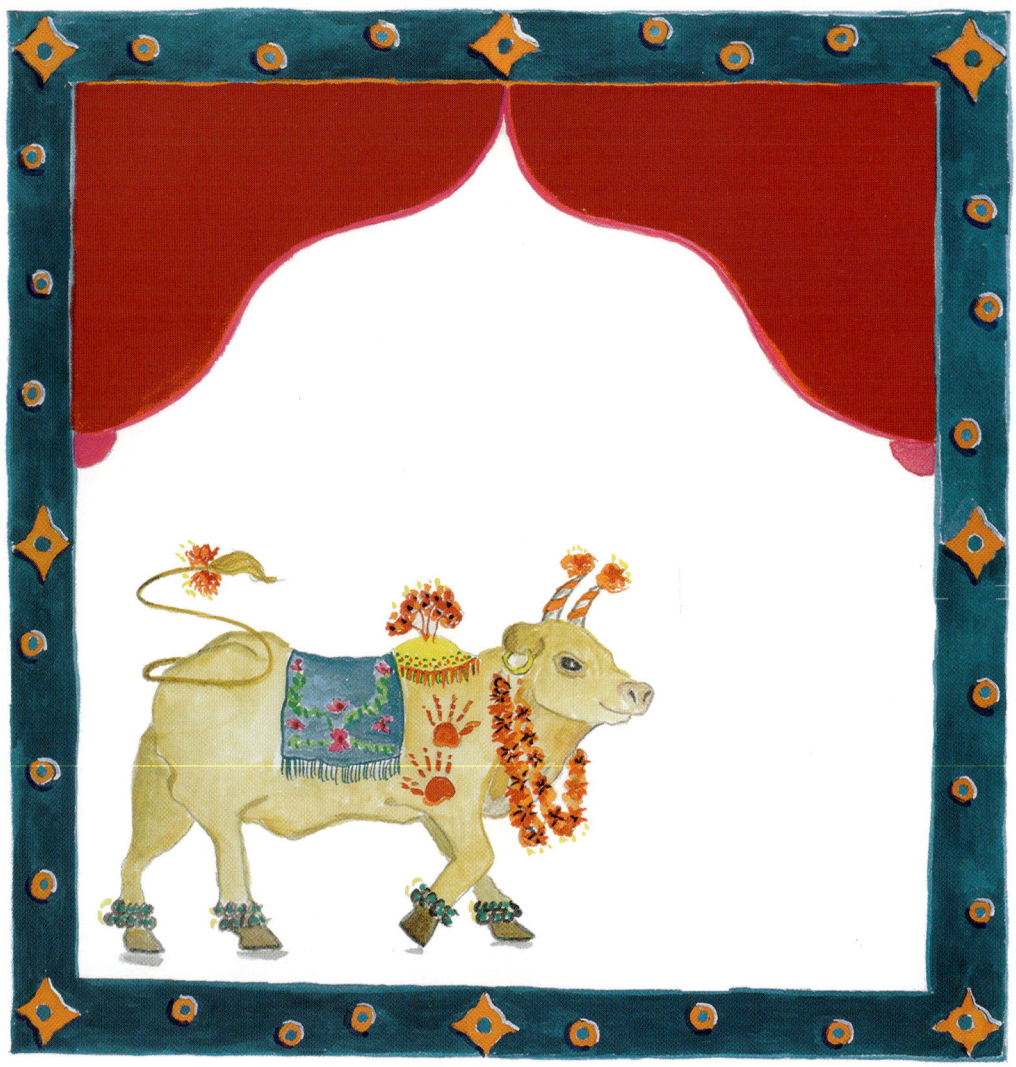

- They also believed in *ahimsā*, or nonviolence, the idea that all living creatures deserve respect.
- Some early Hindus were **ascetics**. This means that they believed in denying their desires, including in some cases the desire to eat meat.

Most, but not all, Hindus are vegetarians. Today about 80% of India's population are Hindus, most practicing some form of vegetarianism.

Buddhism

In 563 B.C., Siddhartha Gautama, the man who would come to be called the Buddha, was born in a small kingdom in Northeast India. Gautama was born into the lap of luxury, but he was deeply disturbed by the misery and poverty he saw outside the walls of his home. While he was still a young man, he left his family and went to search for spiritual understanding.

At first he tried the ascetic way, eating so little (just a few drops of bean soup every day) that he became very thin and sick. He must have been close to death when he decided that asceticism was not the answer.

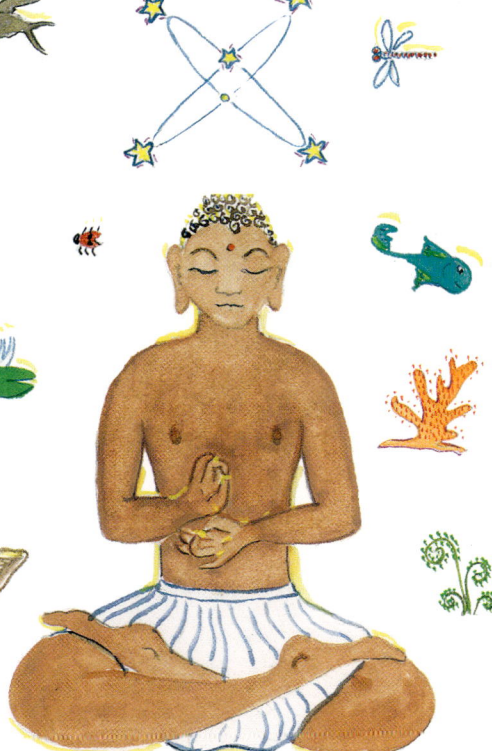

Then he sat down under a tree and meditated for seven weeks. As he meditated, he remembered all the other beings—animals, insects and invisible creatures—his soul had inhabited before it entered his human body. At the end of this meditation, he had achieved enlightenment (he was united with God or the universe) and became, to millions of followers, the Buddha, which means *The Enlightened One*. He recommended that his followers take "the middle path" between self-denial and luxury. He urged them to be non-violent and to respect all life, human and animal alike. Among Buddha's followers, some became vegetarians while others didn't. Today vegetarianism is practiced by many Buddhists, especially in China and Japan.

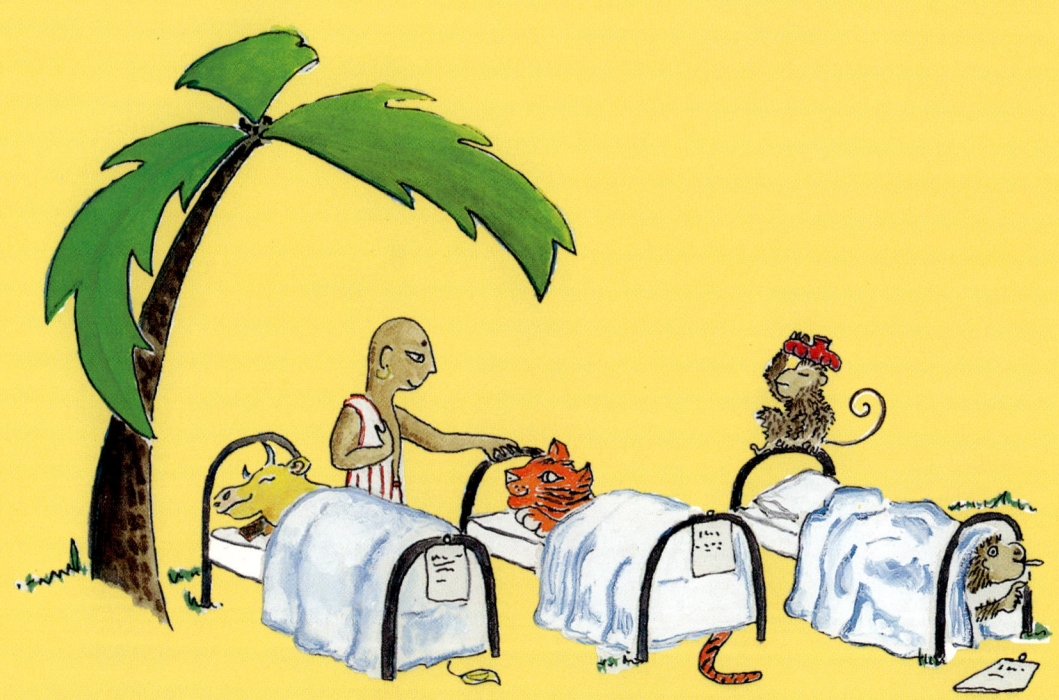

Emperor Asoka

The Emperor Asoka reigned in India during the third century B.C. Early in his reign, he visited a battlefield and was so upset by the soldiers' pain and suffering that he converted to Buddhism. From then on he banished war and embraced the vegetarian way of life. He banned animal sacrifice and slaughter and even built hospitals for sick animals.

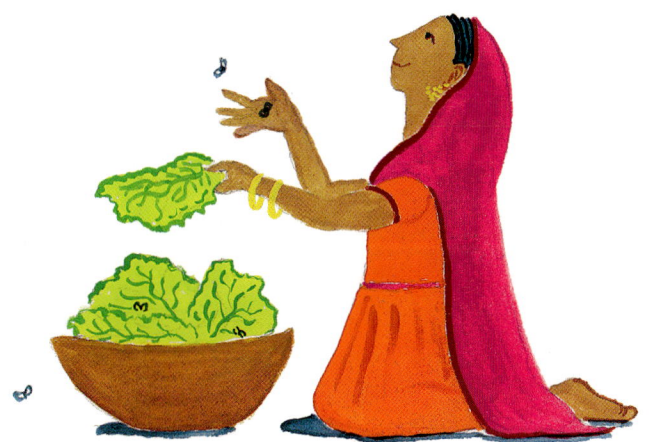

Jainism

The Jains—members of a small Indian religious group—are probably the strictest vegetarians in the world.

Jains say that every living creature—and they include rocks and stones as well as animals and plants!—deserves our respect. They never eat animals of any kind. They even take great care to avoid killing or accidentally eating insects. A Jain housewife will carefully pick through her vegetables to make sure she removes and sets free any bugs that are living on them before cooking the vegetables.

Traditionally, Jain priests wear gauze masks over their faces to avoid inhaling bugs and carry brooms with them to sweep the ground in front of them to avoid stepping on any tiny creatures.

Other religions

The vast majority of Moslems, Christians and Jews are meat-eaters. But there are exceptions. According to a vegetarian reading of the Bible, the first humans—Adam and Eve—were vegetarians. It was only after they sinned and were cast out of the Garden of Eden that they, and all their descendants, began to eat meat. Some vegetarians model their diets on Adam and Eve's.

Jesus, of course, ate meat—he joined in traditional Jewish meals like Passover—but he also taught non-violence. Many Christian vegetarians believe that giving up meat is one way of practicing non-violence. Many Quakers give up meat for this reason.

Other Christians—like

31

Trappist monks—give up meat as a way of purifying their bodies.

In the nineteenth century, many protestant religions—like Seventh Day Adventism, for example—recommended giving up meat and alcohol as a way of cleansing the body and preparing for Jesus's second coming.

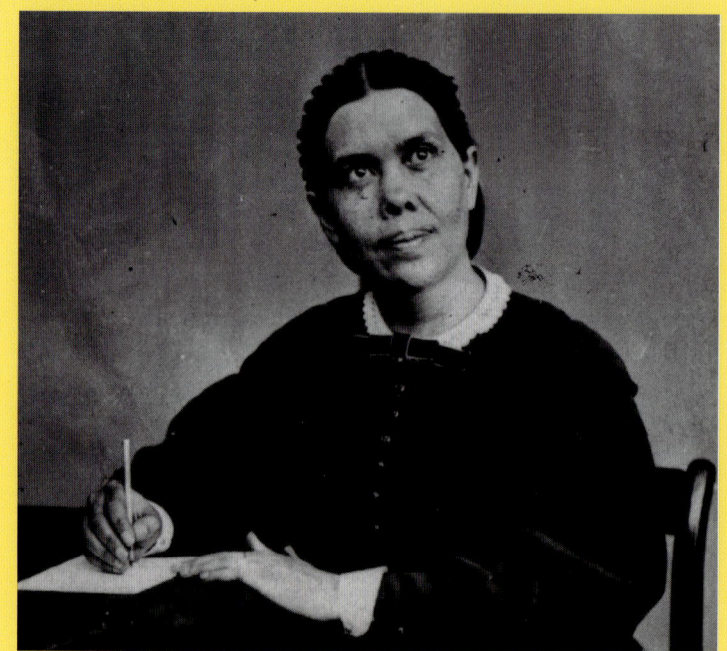

Courtesy of Ellen G. White Estate, Inc.

Ellen White

Ellen White was a woman of vision. She was born in New England in the 1820s, at a time when many people believed the end of the world and Judgment Day (when Jesus would return to determine who went to heaven and hell) were fast approaching. Over the course of her lifetime, she had many visions, which told her that in order to prepare for the coming of the Lord people should give up alcohol, tobacco, tea, coffee and meat and reduce their intake of eggs, butter and cheese. She married a young minister named James White and together they helped to form the Seventh Day Adventist church. They moved to Battle Creek, Michigan, where they built the Health Reform Institute. There, wealthy patients came for treatments that emphasized a healthy lifestyle, including a vegetarian diet.

Food for thought: Vegetarian philosophy

Many of the world's great philosophers, intellectuals and creative writers have been vegetarians.

Pythagoras

The founder of western vegetarianism was Pythagoras, a Greek who was born around 580 B.C., just twenty-odd years before the Buddha. These days, Pythagoras is better known as a mathematician than a vegetarian. (If you've been studying geometry at school, you've probably already made the acquaintance of the Pythagorean Theorem.) But for more than two thousand years he was best known for what he ate. In fact, the word *vegetarian* only came into use in the 1800s—before that, people who didn't eat meat were said to follow a Pythagorean Diet.

A brilliant young scholar, Pythagoras left home to travel the world, studying

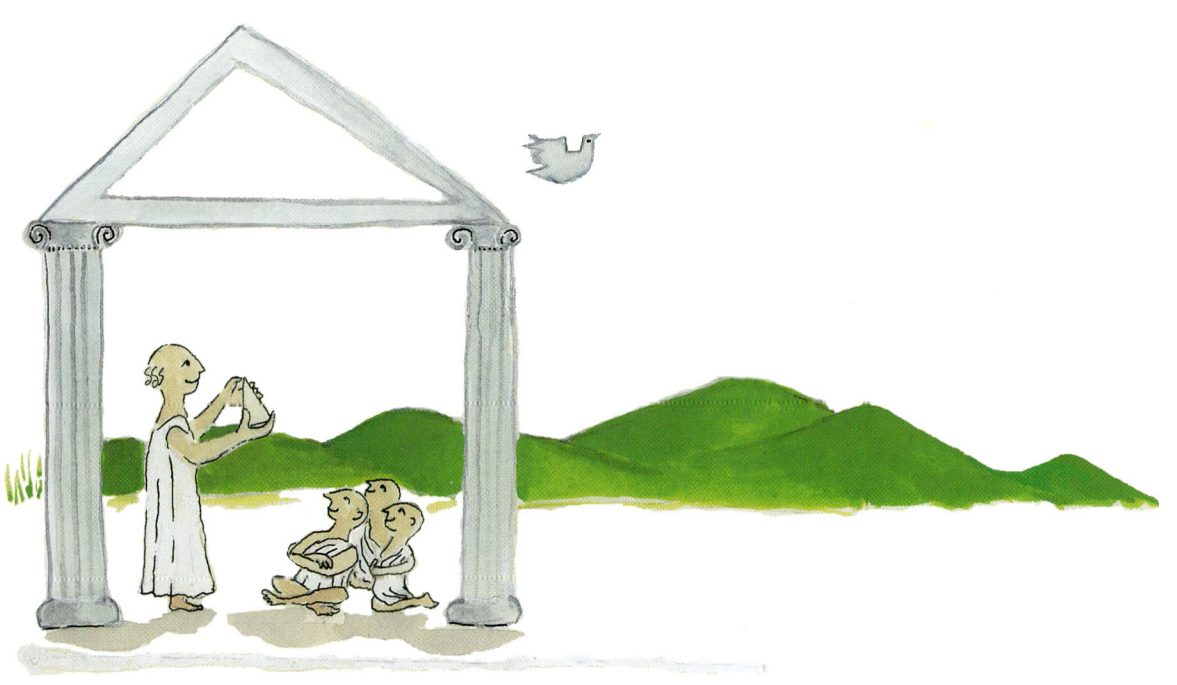

Pythagoras
(c. 582 – c. 507 B.C.)

mathematics, religion and science. After forty years, he settled in the Greek city of Croton and began teaching his new philosophy. Like the Hindus (whose teachings he may have picked up on his travels), Pythagoras claimed that souls were immortal and could inhabit animals as well as people. It was a short step from this theory to the recommendation that human beings refuse to kill or eat animals.

Leonardo da Vinci

From about the time of Jesus until the fifteenth century, Pythagoras and his ideas were all but forgotten. But one "Renaissance Man" who may have learned about his teachings was the painter, anatomist and inventor Leonardo da Vinci. Da Vinci was a passionate vegetarian who believed that killing animals was morally wrong. He used to buy caged birds at the market just so he could set them free. In his notebooks he made many remarks about the rights of animals.

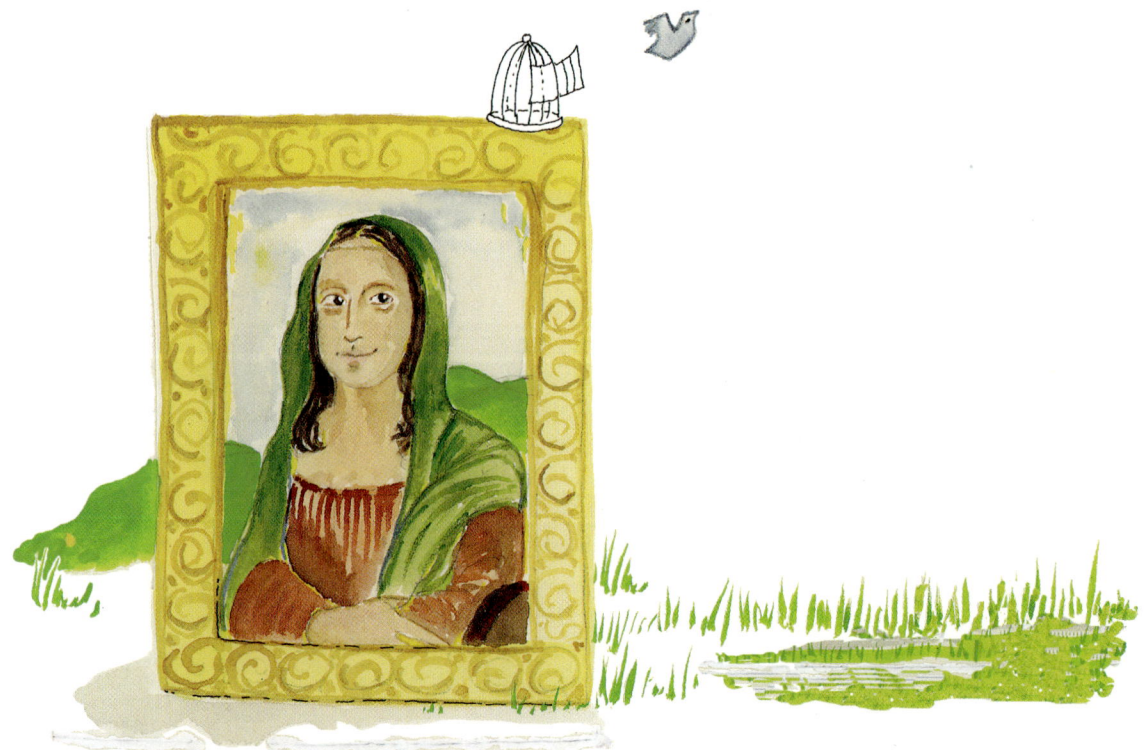

Leonardo da Vinci (1452 – 1519) painted one of the world's best-known works of art, the Mona Lisa.

A Golden Age

The late nineteenth century has been called the *Golden Age of Vegetarianism.* This was a time when many brilliant thinkers turned their minds to questions of human rights, poverty, war, sexism, racism and other burning social problems. It occurred to some of these thinkers that meat-eating, also, might be wrong. Among the famous men and women who embraced the "Pythagorean System" at that time were the poet Percy Bysshe Shelley, the playwright George Bernard Shaw and the Russian novelist Leo Tolstoy. In 1847, the word *vegetarian* was coined and the first Vegetarian Society was formed in England.

Gandhi

Unlike the Europeans who converted to vegetarianism, Mohandas Gandhi was raised to be a vegetarian. He was born into an Indian Hindu family in 1869. At that time, India

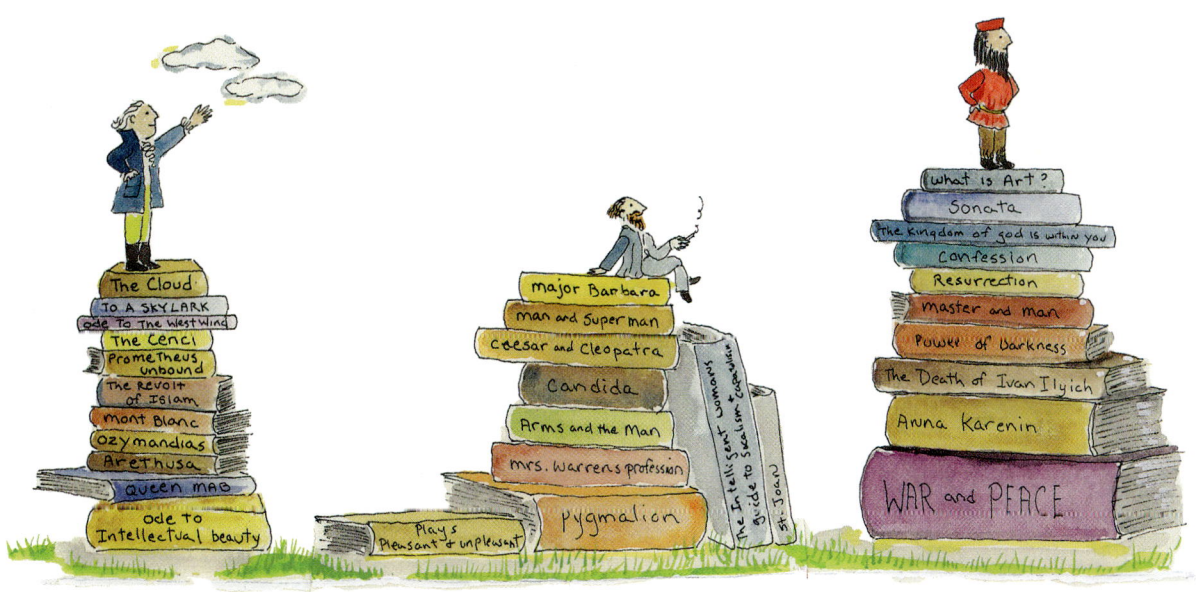

Percy Bysshe Shelley
(1792 – 1822)

George Bernard Shaw
(1856 – 1950)

Leo Tolstoy
(1828 – 1910)

was a colony of England. Many Indians, like Gandhi, longed for independence from England.

In 1888, Gandhi traveled to England to study law. He promised his mother that he wouldn't eat any meat. Aboard ship, he was too shy to ask which foods contained animal products, so he stayed in his cabin and ate through the supply of fruits and sweets he had brought along with him. Once in London, he was almost constantly hungry until by chance he came across a vegetarian restaurant.

At that point in English history, vegetarianism went hand in hand with pacifism, the belief that all war is evil. During his stay in England, Gandhi and his vegetarian friends discussed ways of fighting for civil liberty without using violence.

From England, Gandhi traveled to South Africa where he won civil rights for Indians living there. Finally returning to India, Gandhi taught Indians to use passive resistance—refusal to cooperate with the authorities—and helped stage a peaceful revolution. In the midst of the violence and destruction of the twentieth century, Gandhi proved to the world that there is another way.

Unfortunately…

Of course, the fact that someone is a vegetarian doesn't mean he or she is necessarily a great person. In case you want proof, consider the identity of an on-again-off-again vegetarian who described people who eat meat as "corpse-eaters." That infamous vegetarian was Adolf Hitler.

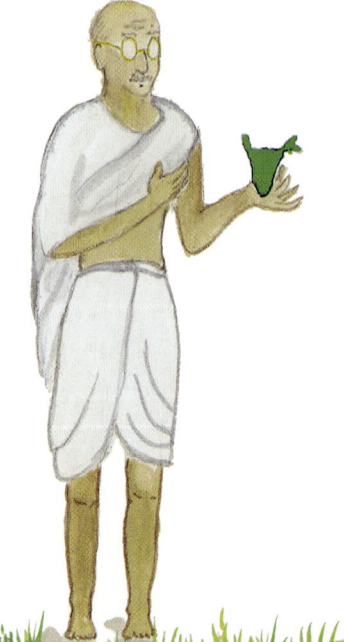

Mohandas Gandhi (1869 - 1948)

Health food: Modern vegetarians

In America in the 1800s, the first "health food nuts" were men and women who believed that giving up meat was the first step toward a purer body. You might recognize the names of two of America's founding fathers of vegetarianism: Sylvester Graham and John Harvey Kellogg. Mr. Graham's name might have appeared on the box of rectangular brown crackers you ate in nursery school, and there's a good chance that you ate a bowl of Mr. Kellogg's cereal for breakfast this morning.

Graham

Sylvester Graham was a Presbyterian minister who traveled around America preaching about the virtues of an alcohol- and meat-free lifestyle. He also recommended hard mattresses, cold showers and a diet based on natural foods. He argued that white, refined flour was bad for you and instead recommended a whole wheat flour that is

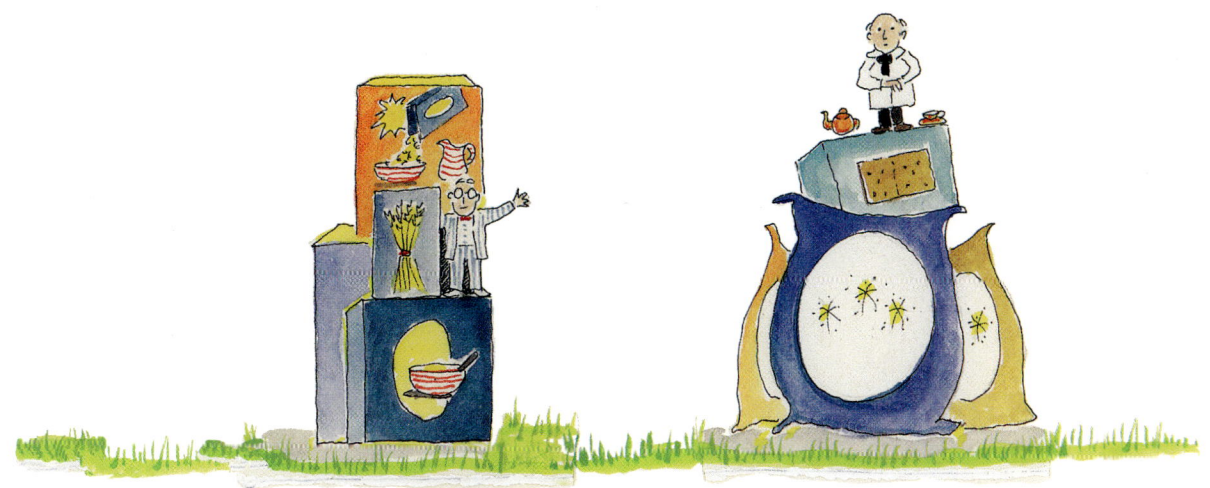

John Harvey Kellogg
(1852 – 1943)

Sylvester Graham
(1794 – 1851)

still called Graham flour today. On at least one occasion, he was attacked by angry butchers and bakers who wanted him to stop interfering with their business.

Kellogg

John Harvey Kellogg was the son of Seventh Day Adventist parents and was therefore raised a vegetarian. When he left his home in Michigan to study medicine in New York, he had to make his own vegetarian meals using grains and nuts. After he became a doctor, he returned to Battle Creek, Michigan to practice. He insisted that his patients adopt a meat-free diet and invented—among other delicacies—peanut butter and corn flakes. John Harvey's brother, Will Kellogg, started the company that still sells John Harvey's invention.

A New Golden Age

Vegetarianism seems to have lost its appeal during the first part of the twentieth century but in the last few decades, it has come back strong. The 1960s and '70s were a time very much like the *Golden Age of Vegetarianism* in the 1800s—a time when many people were raising questions about the way we live our lives. There was a new anti-war movement as well as growing concern about poverty, racism, sexism and other social ills.

Vegetarian issues were raised again. In 1971, Frances Moore Lappé published *Diet for a Small Planet*, a little book that created a big change in the way people eat. She described the ways in which too much meat-eating is bad for people's health, destroys the environment and adds to world hunger.

In 1975, Peter Singer published *Animal Liberation*, a shocking description of the way animals are treated on farms, at slaughterhouses and in research laboratories.

Although vegetarians are still the exception to the rule in mostly meat-eating America, many people have cut back on their meat eating and the vegetarian way of life has become accepted in American society. You may not be able to find a vegetarian selection at your favorite fast-food restaurant, but you're not likely to be attacked by angry butchers if you say you don't eat meat!

Vegetarianism and nonviolence

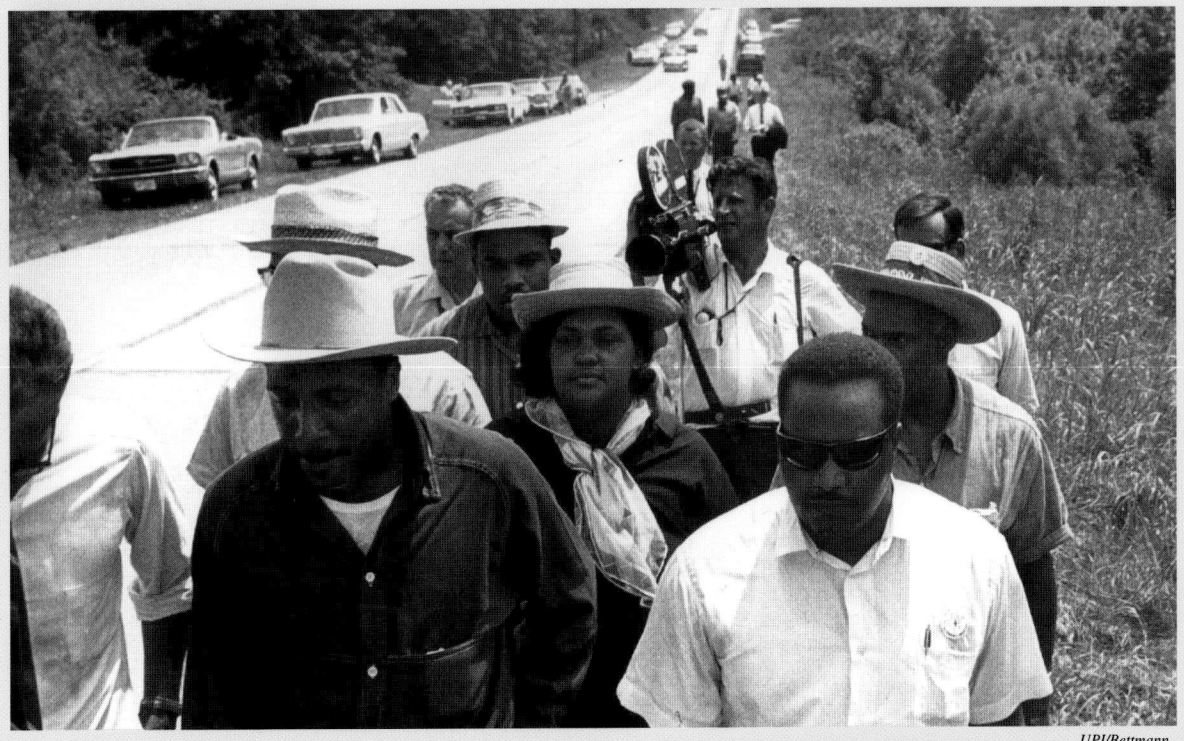

UPI/Bettmann

Dick Gregory, in dark shirt at front left, is shown in 1966 as he starts his march to Memphis, from the spot where James Meredith was shot in Mississippi. With Gregory is his wife, Lillian, about five friends and a dozen newsmen.

"I became a vegetarian in 1965. I had been a participant in all of the major and most of the minor civil rights demonstrations of the early sixties, including the march on Washington and the Selma to Montgomery march. Under the leadership of Dr. King, I became totally committed to nonviolence, and I was convinced that nonviolence meant opposition to killing in any form. I felt the commandment "Thou shalt not kill" applied to human beings not only in their dealings with each other—war, lynching, assassination, murder, and the like—but in their practice of killing animals for food or sport. Animals and humans suffer and die alike. Violence causes the same pain, the same spilling of blood, the same stench of death, the same arrogant, cruel, and brutal taking of life."

from *Dick Gregory's Natural Diet for Folks Who Eat* by Dick Gregory

"About four years ago, when I was six, my mom became a vegetarian. She did it because she didn't want to kill animals and she thinks it's better for the environment. My dad isn't a vegetarian. He says he thinks it's the right thing to do, but since he's been eating meat for so long he can't really stop.

I think being a vegetarian is the right thing to do too but sometimes I eat meat. Like when we go to a Chinese restaurant, I like shrimp-fried rice. Sometimes (not very often) I eat other meat. Like if I'm at a birthday party, I might eat a hamburger. But it bothers me a little — I feel a little guilty.

I like the taste of meat. I miss it. But I'm not happy with myself if I eat a hamburger. It's a living animal and they killed it and I don't think that's right."

Jay Silverman
Age 10
Reisterstown, Maryland

how do vegetarians stay healthy?

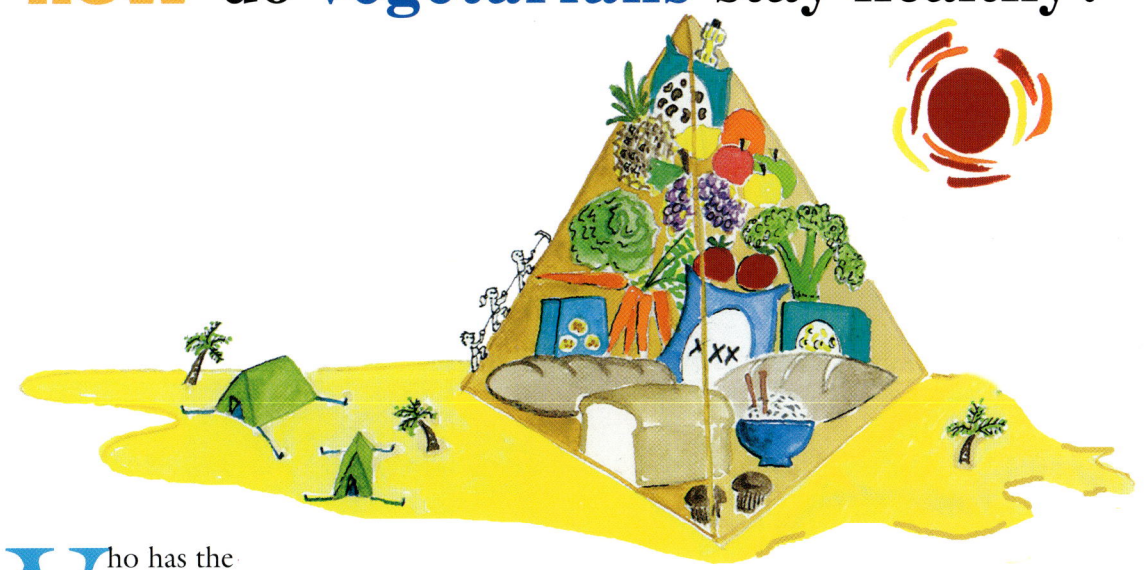

Who has the healthier diet—a vegetarian or a meat-eater? The answer depends on what foods each person eats. A vegetarian who lives on french fries and soda pop eats less healthily than a non-vegetarian who eats a varied diet that includes reasonable portions of lean meat. By the same token, a vegetarian who eats a balanced diet is likely to be healthier than someone who eats a thick slab of prime rib every night. The keys to a healthy diet, whether meat is included or not, are variety and balance.

People have been eating meat for most of human history, so it's natural for meat-eaters to question the value of a vegetarian diet. They may ask: How can you get enough protein if you don't eat meat? How do you get enough calcium if you don't drink milk? How can you get other essential minerals and vitamins, like zinc, iron and Vitamin B12, without eating meat and animal products?

These are excellent questions. Non-vegetarians are right to be concerned about protein and calcium and the other vitamins and minerals normally found in meat. Vegetarians—especially vegans who eat no milk products or eggs—have to be careful to be sure they eat enough of the right kinds of foods.

chapter 5

Every body needs…

Protein is an essential part of every cell in your body. There is protein in your bones, skin, muscles and vital organs. It's the building material that keeps your body strong. Your body can't store protein, so you need to eat something containing protein every day. (Still, the importance of protein can be exaggerated—most Americans eat at least twice as much as they need.) The most common way to get protein is by eating meat but there is plenty of protein in non-meat foods like dairy products, tofu, certain vegetables, grains and beans.

Calcium is a mineral which is important for maintaining strong bones and teeth. Without enough calcium, your bones would start to break down. Children and teenagers need lots of calcium because their bodies are growing and they need calcium to grow strong bones and teeth.

The easiest way to get calcium is by drinking milk or eating milk products like yogurt and cheese. Calcium is found in other foods, too, like leafy green vegetables. There are also calcium-fortified foods, like some soy milks and orange juice.

Riboflavin, zinc, and other nutrients commonly found in meat are important too. Most of these can be found in other foods or in vitamin supplements, although the best combinations may be found in animal products. The most controversial vitamin for vegans is B-12. It is very hard to find this essential vitamin outside of animal products. Nutritionists disagree over how much of this vitamin the body needs and where it can be found.

42

Green cuisine

In America, most meals, especially lunch and dinner, are built around meat. You might eat a roast beef sandwich on rye bread with lettuce and tomatoes, or chicken nuggets with macaroni and carrots or pork chops with mashed potatoes and apple sauce. If you simply took away the meat from those meals and didn't substitute another kind of protein, you wouldn't be eating an ideal diet.

In other countries, where less meat is eaten, meals are built around other kinds of protein. A Mexican burrito, made from refried beans inside a tortilla, is a nutritious, meat-free meal. By the same token, a Chinese meal of stir-fried tofu and vegetables over rice is a healthy and protein-rich dish.

Americans, who aren't used to meals that don't include meat, need to do a little extra planning when they first become vegetarians. It's not as complicated as it sounds, though, especially for ovolactovegetarians (the ones who eat milk and eggs). A varied diet that includes plenty of fresh fruits and vegetables, grains and beans along with milk, cheese and eggs will provide plenty of protein and other nutrients.

Vegans (the vegetarians who don't eat eggs or dairy products) have to work harder to make sure they get enough protein and other nutrients.

Many vegetarians are health-conscious people who like to experiment with non-traditional foods like tofu (made from soy beans), brown rice and bulgar wheat. But you don't have to be wildly experimental to eat healthy vegetarian meals. Macaroni and cheese, peanut butter and jelly sandwiches with a glass of milk and minestrone soup are examples of more traditional meals that are also healthy vegetarian food.

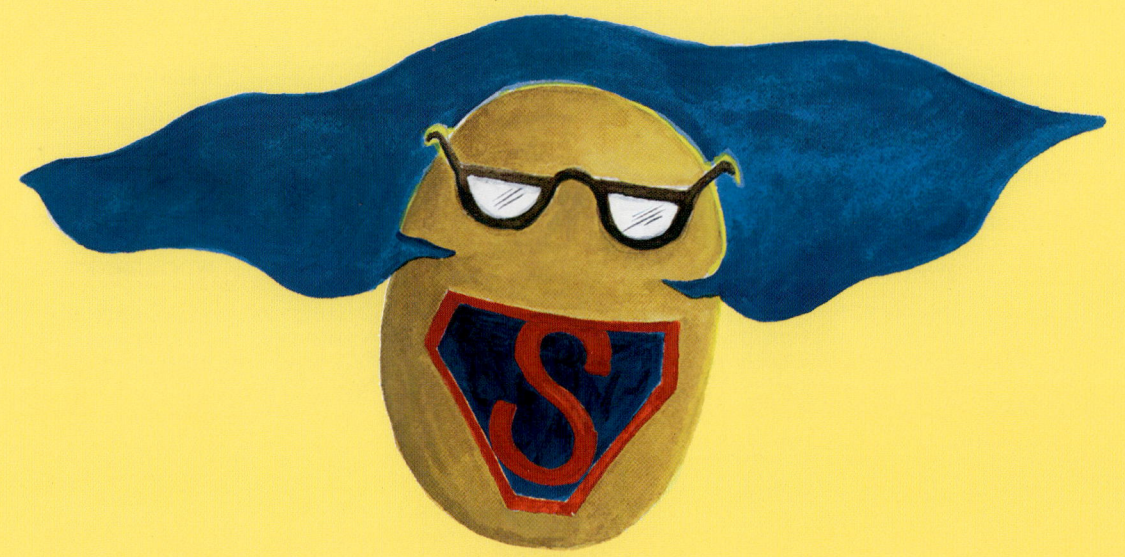

It's a curd! It's a bean! It's Super Soy!

Hundreds of years before the first tofuburger sizzled on an American backyard barbecue, people in China, Japan, Korea and other parts of Asia were harvesting and eating soybeans. This amazing plant is extremely protein-rich. In fact, there's as much protein in a cup of cooked soybeans as there is in three hot dogs, two and a quarter cups of milk or one quarter-pound hamburger!

Americans discovered soybeans in the 1800s and have been growing them ever since—soybeans are our third leading crop after corn and wheat.

Soymilk, especially when fortified with calcium, is an excellent substitute for cow's milk. Tofu, or bean curd, which is made from soymilk, can be cooked in stir-fry dishes, mixed into salads or used in lots of other ways. Some manufacturers have come up with "meat analogues"—foods that taste and look like hamburger, bacon, chicken, ham and other meat dishes but are really made with soybeans.

Vegetarian children

Children and teens are the fastest-growing section of the vegetarian population. Although they have a great deal in common with adult vegetarians, young vegetarians have different needs and different concerns.

It is certainly possible for school-age children and teenagers to eat properly on a vegetarian diet, especially one that includes eggs and milk products. But because children are growing they have different dietary needs from adults. Young vegetarians need to learn about nutrition, consult their doctors and consider taking vitamin supplements to make sure they get enough nourishment. Some studies have shown that the vegan diet (no milk or eggs) may be harmful to babies and young children. So young vegans must be especially careful to eat properly.

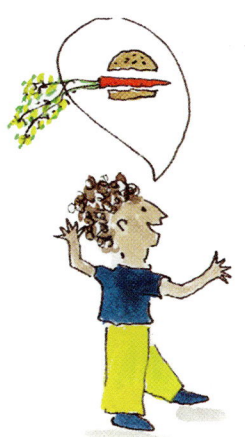

Getting along with parents

Some parents, especially vegetarian parents, are glad when their children decide to become vegetarians. Others are less thrilled. Parents are responsible for their children's health and well-being, so it's natural for them to be concerned when their children change their eating habits. It helps for children to talk calmly with their parents, to show their parents that they're prepared to eat sensibly and to ask their parents to learn more about vegetarianism.

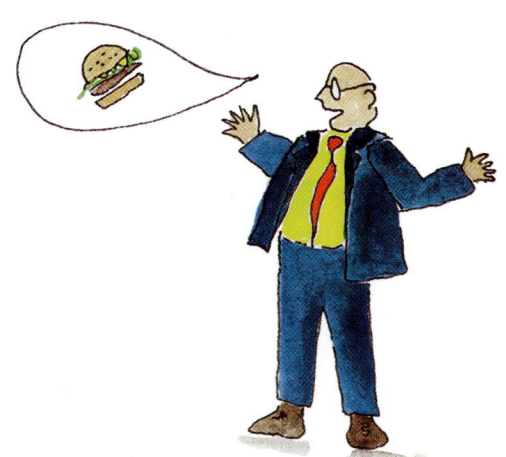

Living in a meat-eating culture

So many traditional kids' foods—like hamburgers, hot dogs, fried chicken—are made of meat that it can be hard for vegetarian children to find something to eat when they're away from home. It helps to tell friends and their parents early on that you're a vegetarian. Away from home, it's a good idea to bring your own meal or to "eat around" the meat—a hamburger bun with lettuce, tomato and cheese, for instance. If you're lucky, your hosts will serve pizza, a popular kids' meal that's also a wholesome vegetarian choice.

Did you know?

That some paint brushes are made from animal hair? That your down sleeping bag is filled with feathers? That your soap could contain animal fat? Here are some of the everyday items that contain animal products:

Clothing: You know that fur coats are made from animals. But what about shoes? Many shoes, boots, belts, coats and other articles of clothing are made from suede and leather, which come from the hides of cattle. Other clothing that is made from animal products includes: down-filled parkas and vests, clothes made of silk, wool, alpaca, angora, cashmere, mohair and felt.

Bedding: Quilts and sleeping bags may be filled with down. Blankets may be made of wool.

Alcoholic drinks: Many wines and beers use small amounts of gelatins and other products.

Medicines: Many medicines are made with gelatins and other animal products too.

Fine china: Fine china is often made from ground animal bones.

Brushes: Animal hair may be used to make paint brushes or shaving brushes.

Gum: Chewing gum is often made with glycerine, another animal product.

Soap and Candles: Both are often made from animal fat.

Cosmetics and perfume: Many cosmetics and perfumes contain animal products. Still more are tested on animals.

Fortunately for strict vegetarians, all of the products mentioned above can be made without harming animals. There are even companies that make "vegetarian" shoes and boots out of polyester and polyurethane that look just like leather.

What's in a name?

You can't always tell by a food's name exactly what's in it. For example, suppose you were a visitor from another planet and someone offered you a "hot dog"—you might think they were offering to cook up the family pet! We use lots of words that disguise the true identity of the animals we eat, like "poultry" for chicken, turkey and other birds and "pork" for pigs. In case you're confused, here's a who's who of meats:

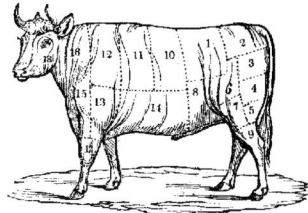 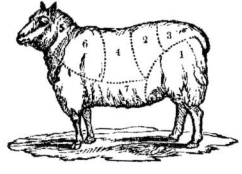 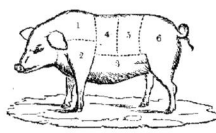 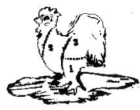

BEEF (cattle) and VEAL (calves)

hamburgers
meatballs
steak
pastrami
roast beef
prime rib
meat loaf
meat balls
hot dogs
corned beef hash

LAMB (young sheep) and MUTTON (full-grown sheep)

lamb chops
leg of lamb
lamb stew
shish-kebob

PORK (pigs)

hot dogs
pork chops
bacon
sausage
ham
roast pork
salami
spare ribs
sweet and
   sour pork

POULTRY (domestic fowl which includes chicken, duck, goose and turkey)

chicken
   nuggets
drumsticks
roast chicken
fried chicken
turkey burgers

About the author

Ellen Klavan's previous books include *The Creative Lunch Box* and *Taming the Homework Monster*. She has written extensively on child care and nutrition for many major magazines.

About the illustrator

Adrienne Hartman has most recently illustrated *The Children's Travel Journal*, for The Little Bookroom, and *Why Can't A Man Be More Like A Cat?* This is her third book.

Printed on acid free paper